THE PERSONAL FINANCE CHOICE
FOR TEENS & YOUNG ADULTS

COMPREHENSIVE GUIDE TO MASTER MONEY
MANAGEMENT & GAIN FINANCIAL
INDEPENDENCE, EVEN WHAT THEY DIDN'T
TEACH YOU IN HIGH SCHOOL

ROBERT F. NEWKIRK JR.

In Memory of:

My Brother of 23 Years, my Business Partner, and a Beloved Pastor:

Rev. Melvin Milton Maxwell

23 May 1961 thru 30 March 2024

TABLE OF CONTENTS

Preface   7
Introduction   9

PART ONE
THE CONSEQUENCES OF FINANCIAL ILLITERACY
1. Understanding the High School Financial Literacy
   Gap   17
2. Capitalism and Financial Illiteracy   31
3. The Battle Against Consumerism   47

PART TWO
BUILDING A STRONG FINANCIAL EDUCATION (AGES 15–18)
4. Financial Literacy 101 for Teens   65
5. The Power of Saving, Investing, and Compound
   Interest   85

PART THREE
TRANSITIONING INTO ADULTHOOD (AGES 19–22)
6. Saving for College and Managing Student Loans   101
7. Managing Limited Income and Expenses   115
8. Smart Spending Habits While Navigating Peer
   Pressure   125
9. Tackling Student Loans and College Costs   135

PART FOUR
ENVISIONING THE FUTURE (AGES 23–28)

10. College Graduation to Career Planning 149
11. Conquering the Fear of the Future 169
12. Saving for Milestones, 1st Car, 1st House, and Family 183
Conclusion: The Personal Finance Choice Is Yours 201

References 205

PREFACE
JUMP INTO THE POOL!!

Jump into the exhilaration of financial freedom! When everything else seems stagnant, plunge into the pool and let the thrill of a cannonball surge through your veins! Feel the instant shift as you propel yourself forward, leaving behind hesitation and embracing the present. Standing on the edge (*the triangle of capitalism, consumerism, and financial illiteracy*), there is no looking back (*the death trap of society*) —only forward into the unknown depths below. To get out of that past state, it is necessary to propel yourself forward, embrace the present, and prepare yourself to hit the pool (*this book, The Personal Finance Choice!*). With a deep inhale, you plunge into a world of liquid tranquility, your senses fully attuned to the here and now (*submerge into the practical advice, actionable strategies, and real-life examples*). As your body melds with the water, every worry fades away, replaced by a serene connection to the aquatic realm (*financial literacy*). Submerged in its embrace, time stands still, and the world above evaporates into insignificance. Then, as you resurface, reborn anew, the world feels different—alive with endless possibilities. Embrace the rush, embrace the new beginnings that await beneath and above the surface!

What does jumping into the pool have to do with finances? It requires courage, determination, and a willingness to embrace the unknown to jump cannonball-style into a world of possibilities. It can be hard to swim if you don't know the basics, and that is where this book comes in—it will help you navigate the sometimes choppy waters of personal finance. The topics in this book identify the triangle mentioned above and call it out for what it is. What can you do about it as a teenager, a college student, and a career-emerging young adult to overcome the systemic traps associated with it? We don't want you to just be able to float and get by, but swim with authority and in the direction that you choose. Instead of the bleak future your past projected onto you, this book will have you prepared to battle capitalism, consumerism, and financial illiteracy head-on! Become the Michael Phelps of money management!

So, are you ready to take the plunge? Are you ready to embrace the opportunities?

Then it is time to JUMP INTO THE POOL!

INTRODUCTION

"When are you going to grow up?" This is a rhetorical question that every teenager and young adult has faced in their lives. It's loaded with so much ammunition as if it serves as a rite of passage question that allows us to be considered a part of society's order of "adulthood." Every young person craves membership—the honor even—of being a part of this society and being recognized as an adult. Yet, we don't know if the requirements and conditions for entry have changed from 20 years ago.

What are the requirements to achieve adulthood? The term has such a vast reach into conditions and time. Some would say we must become mature, virile, fully grown, or fully developed. How subjective is that? Are we referring to physically, mentally, economically, or spiritually? Or is it something else?

Does the term "young adult" mean having a probationary period before being classified as a "full adult"? Is that fair for everyone?

Tradition has set forth some parameters for adulthood that everyone in society tries to adhere to regardless of their age.

- **Physical:** The ability to impregnate, procreate, and feed life in its new environment.
- **Mental:** The fortitude to receive enough education to make life-oriented and career decisions when facing adverse situations.
- **Economical:** The ability to earn enough capital to own a home and provide for a family.
- **Spiritual:** Aware enough to understand relationships with the supernatural and things out of our control.

Society has decided the physical requirement of reaching adulthood is when one turns 18. The mental qualifications fall somewhere between graduating from high school, entering college, or participating in a trade school and getting a job. Oddly, economic rites of passage into adulthood somehow center around the ability to own our own homes! Spiritual maturity comes somewhere in accepting or rejecting our religion and recognizing that the world is not centered around our own state of being.

Mae Jemison (n.d.), the first Black female astronaut once said, "Greatness can be captured in one word: lifestyle. Life is God's gift to us, style is what we make of it." Hmm! From Mae Jemison's quote, the doctrine of adulthood imposes that we acquire a suitable lifestyle which itself requires purchasing some form of home to live in. What happens if there is no housing affordable enough to make the home that we desire?

From as early as the fourth grade, my youngest daughter decided, on her own terms, that she was going to master everything that school had to offer. Boy, did she obtain results! I was so proud of her. She overcame her plateau in mathematics and went on to graduate summa cum laude in high school and proceeded to graduate from Wellesley College during the heart of the COVID-19 pandemic.

That was a monumental task! Since I, as a member of Gen X, had mapped out in my mind what her next steps should be—graduate school or getting a well-paying job in the industry of her study—it appeared to me there was a major shift in her life approach. She, the oldest of Gen Z, decided to stay home for a couple of years working in places like Bed, Bath, and Beyond while attending several K-Pop concerts in different cities along the East Coast.

I realized that, as her father, I no longer had the right to attempt to direct her path; I was now an advisor. All my preconceived thoughts of her next steps in life were shattered. I could only pray that her methods would work as she had my influence from when she was younger. She reached the pinnacle of a young adult and had done exceedingly well up to this point. I kept telling myself it was her life to live. Two years after graduation, she decided to move overseas to Japan to participate in the Japanese English Teacher's (JET) experience.

I was cool with the decision as my oldest daughter, the youngest of the Millennials, had done the same thing and she was returning from Japan at the same time. What threw me off was finding out during her homestay that she had saved over $13,000! (And I thought that she wasn't listening to me and my financial lessons!) She asked me for advice as to what to do with it.

Phew! I was shocked, but relieved!

During our financial discussions, one question kept ringing through my ears with an alert attached to it. She asked me, "What's the point of saving for the future if the future I see ahead looks so bleak?" Wow! My knees buckled when she asked me that question. As difficult as that may be, it is worth touching upon right now, and more details will follow.

If you want to know how people feel about themselves, look at their bank account. Money is the greatest measurement of your mindset. Men and women who possess a stout heart, an unconquerable will, and the determination to push ahead, extend far from poverty whether they have had a loss or not. As John H. Johnson (n.d.), the publisher of *Ebony Magazine* said, "Wealth is less a matter of circumstance than it is a matter of knowledge and choice. You must take control of your life—you must make the decision to be wealthy."

Let's return to the term "lifestyle." To make anything, you need money! Yes, today's real estate environment is not the same as it was 20 years ago. Today's career opportunities, after the pandemic, clearly are not the same as they were 20 years ago. We can also throw in the issues of climate change, inflation, and the unleashed competition between corporations and small businesses. Nevertheless, the answer to my daughter's question is that we still must save money no matter how unpredictable the future may be. We still must give ourselves power in the present.

There is a powerful quote from Dr. W.E.B. Du Bois (n.d.) that says, "Many a ruined man dates his downfall from the day he began buying what he did not need. If you are in debt, part of you belongs to your creditors. To whom you give your money, you give your power."

Our measure of wealth is not defined by the cars we drive or the clothes we wear. Money represents our ability to gain those things in the future, but we need the fortitude to "chase the bag." What bag are you trying to obtain? Is your bag an instant gratification bag or a retirement bag? I would recommend balancing the two which means transferring instant gratification to delayed gratification and obtaining the means to get it.

Perhaps the most shocking statement I've read of late is that a whopping 75% of American teenagers lack confidence in their knowledge of personal finance (Turner, 2023).

Why is personal financial education among teenagers and young adults a figment of the imagination? Did someone forget to fill the void or was it done on purpose? Let me start to fill that void right now. When money starts to fall into your pocket at any given point in time, there are two things to do with it: save it or spend it.

Spending may happen sooner or later for that money, but when it is spent, was it spent wisely? In the current times, if the dollar wasn't spent wisely, then it was spent foolishly! So, for teenager confidence, not knowing the answer to this question probably means that the dollar was spent foolishly!

Finally, the answer to the daunting question presented in our introduction: Not only should we save despite looking at a bleak future, but we must also be tenacious about it!

And this is why I wrote *The Personal Finance Choice for Teens & Young Adults*. I have purposefully curated its content for people aged 15–28 who are aspiring to become independent adults and gain honorary status in the society of adulthood. But this is not another book that points out blatantly obvious means of obtaining adulthood through financial education.

Instead, each of these traditional means will be examined and counted, asking the pertinent question, "How do they still apply in today's current economic climate as it pertains to Millennials and Gen Z, coming from a Gen X point of view?" And yes, some of those traditional elements that may have worked out for Gen X will not necessarily work for Millennials and Gen Z.

This is why it's important to explore alternate solutions that will work for you, the very Millennials and Gen Zs who are hanging themselves out to dry. I personally encourage you to read this book and study the lessons it contains. Identify the points that resonate with you and put them to good use. Create new habits by following the fundamental codes that have been hidden from you until now. And, if you follow this process, you will not only plant the seeds of wealth but also have the knowledge you need to nurture and care for them as you begin to master money management, gain financial independence, and secure your future.

PART ONE
THE CONSEQUENCES OF
FINANCIAL ILLITERACY

When someone betrays your intelligence and trust,
"JUMP INTO THE POOL!"
That forces us to move into the next moment.
And when you get out of the pool, FIGURE it out!

CHAPTER 1
UNDERSTANDING THE HIGH SCHOOL FINANCIAL LITERACY GAP

The State of Financial Education in High Schools: Understanding the Gap

F irst, let me say that it is not your fault. The burden rests on people like you and me, but that is not the root of it. The root is a systemic issue and evidence shows that most Americans are tired of being complacent about their financial literacy and are looking for ways to overcome it. In fact, high school students are becoming increasingly interested in financial education, with a colossal 73% of teens reporting wanting more financial education in 2023 (Turner, 2023).

From 2018 to 2022, we see a steady incline in the number of students taking a personal finance course, particularly a 6.3% rise. However, financial education in the United States is yet to catch up to the demand. In fact, less than 10% of students have access to a personal finance course in states where financial education is not mandated. No wonder many of our students are frightened by their future financial possibilities. Only eight states (Alabama, Iowa, Mississippi, Missouri, North Carolina, Tennessee, Utah, and

Virginia) have fully implemented personal finance courses for high schoolers, and fifteen (Connecticut, Florida, Georgia, Indiana, Kansas, Louisiana, Michigan, Minnesota, Nebraska, New Hampshire, Ohio, Oregon, Rhode Island, South Carolina, and West Virginia) are in the process of fully implementing the courses. Only 23 of the 50 states have verbally committed to having the ball rolling at some point in the distant future (Next Gen Personal Finance, 2023). That means less than half of the states are currently teaching financial education in high schools! I meant what I said—it is not you!

Why High Schools Fail to Teach Financial Literacy

The following 2023 financial statistics should prompt action from our policymakers:

- Twenty-five percent of Americans reported having no one to turn to for financial advice or guidance.
- Sixty percent of non-retirees reported having zero confidence that their retirement savings were in order.
- Forty-one percent of teenagers don't know what a 401(k) is and 32% of them don't know the difference between a debit card and a credit card (Louis, 2024).

It is important to acknowledge that there are some experts and professionals who are pushing against the implementation of financial literacy studies in high schools because they believe that the efforts are redundant and have little to zero effects on people's behaviors with money. This class of experts, obviously, comes from an old-school line of thought that only through pain can people change their financial behaviors. Norman Finkelstein said in an interview that there is a billionaire class that is attempting to stifle academic freedom at major universities that have three of the first-ever female presidents (Harvard, MIT, and University of Pennsylvania) by toppling them with charges and making them resign (Finkelstein, 2023).

They have been successful with two of them. President Liz Magill (University of Pennsylvania), resigned amid controversies over antisemitism. It was said during her hearing at Capitol Hill that if they were to succeed in making her step down, and they did, it would set a catastrophic precedent in academia.

President Claudine Gay (Harvard) also resigned amid controversies over antisemitism, which narrowed down to allegations of plagiarism. She wrote that she hoped her resignation would "Deny demagogues to further weaponize my presidency to undermine the ideals animating Harvard since its founding" (Gay, 2024).

If a billionaire class can say, "We are going to withdraw a $50 million donation to a school unless you do what we say," and the schools comply, it sets a catastrophic precedent. If the president of a major university can be overthrown, then they can get rid of courses, faculty, and administration. There is no safe place in academia anymore, and all of this is happening out in the open (Finkelstein, 2023)!

How does this groundbreaking story relate to our topic? We must pay attention as this attack on higher learning easily trickles down to high schools and keeps financial courses out of the classroom. This kind of opposition toward personal finance lessons in schools is real, and it is detrimental to quality personal financial education being delivered to all high schoolers and young adults. This is more reason for us to take matters into our own hands—and gather personal financial knowledge for ourselves and distribute it to our families and our friends.

There is a tremendous amount of power in money, so money has to be rare! Another reason why people are against financial education is that in order to keep most people from having a lot of money, they have to prevent them from understanding money and how it works. If people do not understand how it works, they will not be able to build masses of it. Instead, acquiring money has taken on the characteristics of gambling.

The Consequences of a Lack of Financial Education

Let's look at the current state of debt in America. Currently credit card debt in America amounts to $1.03 trillion, and approximately one-third of adults reported that their paychecks barely cover their basic needs (Wallace, 2023).

Young people aged 18 to 29 years old are in debt on average by $12,871—that's $69 billion total! While this age bracket is far from having the highest debt in America, it is the most concerning since many of them are just starting to enter the workforce. Some of them may not even have jobs yet, like those who have just graduated high school or are still in college.

Imagine having thousands of dollars in debt when you have yet to find or build a stable career! Who is obtaining the power right now? It is so important that we change this fact soon or the future will certainly become bleak. We need to learn how to make smart financial decisions while time is on our side. I firmly believe that prevention is better than cure—that is, it's easier to stay out of debt than get out of it.

Educating young people about personal finance seems common-sensical but there are a continuing number of critics of financial education, nonetheless. For instance, Ogden argued that financial education is a waste of time because it apparently fails to change spending behavior, citing some studies that support his claim. If it did lead to improvements, he added, the results were so low that they were insignificant. While he presented some interesting ideas in his 2019 opinion piece in *The Washington Post,* for example, "Americans' finances are in terrible shape because the cost of higher education, health insurance, childcare, and rent have all increased far faster than paychecks," I still disagree with his overall thesis that financial education is a waste of time (Ogden, 2019).

For the sake of argument, let's say that Ogden was right—the positive impact of financial education is so minuscule that it remains insignificant. Even if this is the case, should we just ignore the people that financial education is helping? Or should we look at the current curriculum, find its blind spots, and make adjustments where improvements can be made so it could help more people make better financial decisions? Evidence shows that the main reason financial education may be ineffective in changing spending behavior is that it fails to address the motive behind the behavior (Menard, 2017). However, if we can somehow draw back the curtains and urge students to examine their tendencies in approaching money, then we can unlock the full potential of financial education and make a real difference in people's lives.

Billy J. Hensley, President and CEO of the National Endowment for Financial Education agrees with my sentiment and says, "If students don't meet standards in math or reading comprehension, should we just give up? No, we pivot. We adjust. We step up our efforts. Achieving financial well-being—much like our overall health—takes a comprehensive approach." He also listed some parameters on what constitutes a high-quality financial education program.

> The framework for competent, purposeful, and lasting interventions is that they are delivered by well-trained educators who are confident delivering the lessons; they include vetted program materials that come from trusted, unbiased sources; they are comprised of timely instruction presented when it can be applied. They contain relevant subject matter that fits the needs of diverse audiences, and they demonstrate evidence of impact and affect behavior change. (Hensley, 2019)

As Hensley said, we can't give up on financial education just because we're currently unsatisfied with its results. Looking at the state of financial education in the country, it's clear that we're still in the early stages of development and there is still a lot of room for improvement. What we need is to create a good curriculum using stable and effective building blocks that not only teach financial skills but also affect behavior change. I agree with Hensley in that the system needs to take a broader focus on what works for individual students and apply it accordingly so that the curriculum can cater to a more diverse group of students.

The alternative is to allow young people to graduate and enter the workforce without a solid foundation in financial literacy and to continue the cycle of debt in the country, which is what our capitalistic society wants. After all, it becomes a whole lot easier for the elite to take money from you if you're not equipped to manage your personal finances.

That said, I am glad that you have decided to educate yourself with this book. I don't know if your school is in one of the eight states where personal finance courses are mandatory, but taking this step is a step in the right direction, nonetheless. Your initiative to learn already proves that you have great potential—it shows your desire to break the cycle and build a brighter future for yourself.

Now that we have a better understanding of the gap in financial education in this country, let's take a closer look at what these sections have to say about the impact of financial illiteracy on young adults.

The Impact on Young Adults

The idea of introducing financial education in high schools has existed for a while; however, it has been met with opposition. A comprehensive meta-analysis journal published in 2013 evaluated the proposed financial literacy program by examining 168 research papers on 201 studies. The conclusion was that financial literacy accounted for a 0.1% behavioral change in the financial habits of individuals, highlighting a much smaller change in those with the lowest incomes (Fernandes et al., 2014).

This is the information that most financial education critics have pointed to against the implementation of financial education in schools. This report has been supported by another study done by the Goethe University of Frankfurt in Germany that concluded that the 0.1% was actually an overestimation and the possibilities of zero impact were much higher. A more recent study report in Germany contradicted the Goethe University conclusion with findings that financial education in teenagers had a similar impact on behavioral changes and learning outcomes as those of other subjects (Bover et al., 2018). Why the critics have continued to ignore the findings of this recent report is baffling.

In consideration of the studies being cited by the critics, the 0.1% impact of financial education is being cited as a result of the fact that the cost of living has skyrocketed. Many Americans are barely meeting their needs with their paychecks. My convictions are that the information from the finance education program was well received but most of these people did not have the financial flexibility to apply these concepts in a manner that would have reflected the true impact of financial literacy.

Reflecting on the conclusion made by Goethe University, the merit of their conclusion that financial literacy had close to zero impact on behavioral changes was based on a financial crash course. This study analyzed nine research papers that focused on students, immigrants, and low-income earners who may benefit the most from the crash course. The argument raised by these scholars was that even though the individuals targeted by the study showed a short-term increase in financial knowledge, it did not guarantee a long-term change in financial behavior. These are my arguments against the conclusions of this study:

- First, we cannot accept or view this as a financial crash course! The term "crash course" is why there is no proven evidence of long-term behavior. A crash course is not designed to provide long-term results.
- Second, let's debate this with the Biblical scripture in the book of Proverbs 22:6: "Train up a child in the way he/she should go, and then when he/she is old, he/she will not depart from it. (New King James Version, n.d.)" This is what is meant by implementing a long-term behavior: Teens are not being taught financial literacy at an early age. Instead, they are being taught that money is a "hot potato." In other words, spend the money as soon as you get your hands on it. The "hot potato" philosophy supports these scholar's findings.
- We must give an alternate approach so that teens know how to hold onto money and create investment opportunities. Stop using crash courses as an excuse and start teaching financial education as every person deserves to be taught.

The Urgent Need for Change

Dennis P. Kimbro, author of *The Wealth Choice*, had this to say, "Prosperity begins with the mind but ends in the purse. The sooner you begin, the better!"

Reforming our approach to financial literacy is imperative if we want our future generations to have a fighting chance of success in this society.

The following U.S financial literacy statistics illustrate how important reform is:

- The US ranks 14th in the world on financial literacy. This puts our national literacy rate at 57%, beating Botswana, which recorded 52%, while Canada and Germany recorded 68% and 66% literacy rates respectively.
- Eighty-five percent of students are not required to take financial literacy education.
- Seventy-six percent of Millennials do not have a basic understanding of financial information (Klapper et al., 2015).

The key personal finance questions used by the Financial Industry Regulatory Authority (FINRA) to assess people on their understanding of basic financial facts showed that American citizens have gotten worse at answering them correctly (Klapper et al., 2015).

What are the other countries that are beating the US in financial literacy doing to stay ahead? The need for financial education has been recognized and is being implemented in many different ways by many countries. For example, most countries have realized how ineffective it is to try and use behavioral modification approaches to intervene in people's financial issues.

As explained earlier in the chapter, changing behavior requires the availability and flexibility of options, which most adults lack regarding their financial needs. A new approach based on behavioral development is being implemented and some countries are starting financial education in early primary schools.

To further the urgency and need for change, we must consider the following benefits of teenagers becoming financially literate in their personal lives:

- a basic understanding of the main financial products and which ones to acquire based on personal needs and circumstances
- a practical long-term plan that is less likely to be affected by any abrupt surprises due to lack of money
- a vision for financial independence
- an ability to manage emotional and mental pressures by overcoming their lack of information.

Recommendations to Parents and Guardians

Parents and guardians must consider several additional factors justifying a need for financial education in schools other than the ones that have been mentioned so far. For example, corporate America has transferred pensions over into 401(k) plans where the responsibility of retirement has shifted from the employer to the employee. This move should have been met by an educational policy that adequately prepares the people in the workforce on how to manage their 401(k).

Why did they not offer financial courses to help prepare employees to manage their retirement? Greed! A lack of education on effective planning for retirement means everybody's money is up for grabs by marketing and advertising to the very employees who have not been prepared accordingly. They end up spending potential retirement money foolishly or gaining extensive penalties not understanding the policies of withdrawing retirement money.

I know of several people who lost over $100,000 in penalties to their 401(k) when they were 57 years of age because they were unaware they had to wait until 59 1/2 years of age to withdraw without penalty. The idea of self-awareness and marketing tricks used to take money away from unsuspecting people who work so hard for their money should be at the center of the content of the financial curriculum that should be rolled out.

As parents, we can prevent our teenagers from going through similar financial issues as us by demanding literacy education in high schools. We can play a role and start encouraging our children on how to manage money.

This means getting them involved in budgeting for groceries and developing strategies for cutting down on utility bills. In the United Kingdom, the government recognized schools as the place where they could reach all the people of their society when kids took the financial lessons they learned back to their homes.

Money is very slippery and capitalism in America is a pressure tactic designed to take away consumer's money at a moment's notice. We must prepare to defend against this undertaking. Awareness is key. Are we ready to question the status quo and take the appropriate action?

The next chapter will explain how capitalism is connected to financial illiteracy and expose the financial literacy gap in the school system.

Personal Finance Highlights

1. Urgent Need for Change: The dire state of financial literacy in the United States, afinancial instability plaguing young adults, immediate action is imperative to secure a brighter financial future for all.

2. Impact of Financial Illiteracy: A lack of financial education hampers individuals' ability to make informed decisions about money, manage debt, and plan for the future, with far-reaching consequences. Illustrating real-world implications compels readers to acknowledge the critical importance of addressing financial illiteracy.

3. Roles of Parents and Guardians: Empowering parents and guardians to advocate for financial education in schools is crucial, as it emphasizes their role in fostering financial literacy at home and pushing for curriculum changes. This shift in narrative encourages collective action and community involvement to address the financial education gap.

4. Preparing for the Future: In unraveling the link between capitalism and financial illiteracy, it's clear that awareness and action are vital in safeguarding against predatory financial practices. By challenging norms and promoting comprehensive financial education, we empower individuals to navigate the intricate financial terrain of today and construct a more secure tomorrow.

5. Connection to Capitalism: The chapter links financial illiteracy to systemic issues, particularly within capitalism, highlighting how it exploits financial ignorance and

perpetuates inequality. This prompts readers to challenge the status quo and take proactive steps toward financial empowerment and literacy.

6. Only 23 of the 50 states are currently teaching financial education in high schools!
7. Opposition toward personal finance lessons in schools is real, and it is detrimental to quality personal financial education being delivered to all high schoolers and young adults.
8. There is a tremendous amount of power in money, so money has to be rare!
9. It's easier to stay out of debt than get out of it.
10. Money is very slippery and capitalism in America is a pressure tactic designed to take away consumer's money at a moment's notice.

CHAPTER 2
CAPITALISM AND FINANCIAL ILLITERACY

D id you know that 69% of the wealth in America is held by less than 10% of the population? This means that for every $100 in the economy, one person out of ten gets $69, while the other nine divide the leftover $31 among themselves. Most capitalist societies, like the US, have similar wealth inequalities in their systems. However, gross domestic product (GDP) per capita is a term used by most capitalist nations to mask this wealth inequality. GDP per capita is the total amount of money every American would get if all the money in the economy were to be divided equally. Understanding how capitalism works and how it connects to financial illiteracy will help us formulate healthy financial decisions as a teenager and a young adult.

Capitalism is built on the premise of consumerism: the more people buy, the more money seven percent of the wealthy make. A lot of money and effort from that seven percent has gone into making sure people continue spending. The system encourages selling schemes that give people the idea that the more they accumulate, the more they will find satisfaction, comfort, and fulfillment.

The majority of the American population must solely exist as consumers for capitalism to work efficiently. However, the profits are never enough, so more effort is made through insidious mediums like advertising on TV, radio, magazines, and social media to entice people to spend more, to their financial detriment.

Then as financial illiteracy and classism feed upon each other, capitalism takes center stage and leaves no room for the sound financial reasoning required for financial well-being. This is what teenagers and young adults face when they integrate into society as independents.

What Is Capitalism?

By definition, "capitalism" is a system of trading in which individuals operate to serve their interests and needs with little to no interference from the government. Understanding modern capitalism and its structure is the best way to shield ourselves from its ruthless influences.

This definition goes way back to the 18th century when Adam Smith, a philosopher regarded as the father of modern economics, emphasized that the best way to get what we want is to give someone who has what we want what they want in exchange for something they want.

In today's world, teenagers and young adults are told what they want, and corporations take their money and continue to take more until the person drives themselves deep into debt. Rajan and Zingales once said, "Save capitalism from capitalists," (Rajan, 2003). This statement points to observations made by many professionals—that capitalism has run rampant and serves the agenda of only the seven percent.

The Key Principles of Capitalism

True capitalism is controlled by the people who purchase goods and services owned by businesses and private individuals. Capitalist societies are not controlled by the government, per se, and it's important to have a clear understanding of the principles of capitalism so that we can understand where things have gone wrong for Americans.

Free markets are called laissez-faire capitalism and are defined by an economic structure where private individuals are unrestrained in their buying power. Under this system, we are free to make choices and invest our money into whatever we want. There are no checks or controls in place and any decision made is voluntary as well as decentralized. A key principle of laissez-faire is the *right* to own property and without this right, capitalism is not being properly instituted.

In a capitalist society, the main driving force behind production is demand. When demand for certain goods rises and the supply remains the same, prices increase. It also signals that the producer should make more of the demanded product, increasing their profit. True capitalism reaches an equilibrium state once this demand is met, prices move back down, and the fluctuation between supply and demand adjusts.

As Americans, we live under the illusion that our nation is truly capitalist. The threads of each of the principles of capitalism allude to the fact that we have free choice. We have the right to own property. We have the benefit of choice to engage in trade with others through open competition for goods and services, but when we are denied equal access to financial education, it makes the system unfair.

There are alarmingly high instances and reports of people purchasing a service or product only to find that it is not what they wanted or how it appeared. When they try to return the product, many of these corporations and businesses will roll out tons of information on policies that are difficult to understand. This means that even if an item of property is purchased, many are deprived of their right to *feel* ownership because the product is not what was wanted—nor what was advertised.

Herbert Spencer (n.d.) said, "The great aim of education is not knowledge, but action." This statement speaks volumes when it comes to financial literacy and the insistence of the wealthy in metaphorically dumbing down future generations when it comes to knowing what to do with their money. We're being shown a smoke-and-mirrors act so that the financial gap can continue to widen, while policymakers in Congress continue to "debate" whether financial education is necessary—it is!

Capitalism vs. Other Economic Systems

While there certainly are mixed economies worldwide, it's important to know the underlying threads of each economy. The reason for this is that mixed economies can still be governed by the principles of a specific economic system while implementing some of the principles of another to push a political agenda, ruling party wealth, and so on. An example of this mixed system is China, a country that is ruled by communism, with much of its manufacturing concerns privatized, and a socialist market economy (SME) being driven to ensure enormous control is still present over the economy.

Socialist economies were developed in direct opposition to the abuse of capitalism in the late 18th and early 19th centuries. In Western Europe industrial production compounded economic growth at breakneck speed. Those on one side of capitalism catapulted to riches quickly while the rest of the population descended into poverty at an alarming rate.

Socialist principles include

- production for demand and use rather than profit.
- a more equitable distribution of material resources and wealth.
- a cessation of competitive buying and selling in the marketplace.
- free access to essential goods and services.

In socialist economies, the collective *should* own and control the production of goods and services. The right to personal property is permitted in the form of consumer goods and essential services, like public transport, education, and healthcare are free but funded by taxation. The primary difference between socialist economies and capitalism stems from property rights and the control of production.

Communist economies are the antithesis of capitalistic economies. In a communist economy, property rights are shared—what's yours is mine, and what's mine is yours. The right to private ownership, therefore, doesn't exist. In theory, a communist economy is developed to eliminate the class struggle, creating a balance in which everyone is relegated to somewhat of a social equilibrium. On paper, communist economies sound great, but in reality, they remove the fundamental rights of an individual and hand entirely too much power to government systems.

The absence of incentive to work and produce profit leads to less innovation, less profit as a result of little or no competition, and a general lack of interest in self-welfare. In addition, the concentration of power in the hands of the government leads to inefficiency and a dictatorship. Societies are forced to work for the betterment of the whole, and in the end, the economy and the people themselves end up suffering.

Ironically, communist economies were designed to narrow the inequality gap but only ended up widening it, with the most elite pocketing and profiting from the work of others and the others being ordered to share anything they managed to accumulate.

Of course, inequality exists on some level in any financial system. A windfall, inheritance, and the generation of income through effective strategies all lead to some form of inequality quotient. Having said that, the inequality pointed out in this book is based on the errors within the American capitalist system and not on self-education or luck.

This book is not a communist standpoint of all being equal but rather a deep dive into the tactics being used to stifle the potential financial growth of future generations. It provides you with the tools you need to make *informed* decisions about leveling the financial playing field. More importantly, it's about the education needed to make a choice that is indicative of your *right* to own the property you want throughout your life.

Capitalism and Wealth Inequality

For every $1.7 million the super-wealthy make, regular folks make $1. This statistic comes from the World Economic Forum held in Switzerland (Piette, 2023). The rate of economic inequality is increasing rapidly.

While the more ethical world billionaires suggest that governments impose higher taxes on super-rich and large corporations to curb this growing inequality, the reality is that this solution is only temporary. The reason for this is that wealth inequality needs to be addressed at the systemic root of the problem—the exploitation of workers and consumers.

The World Economic Forum highlights just how dire the shift in wealth from the working class to a newly evolved capitalist class has become but fails to explain how this happened because doing so would go against the agenda of the very capitalist class driving this change. You see, capitalism at its core, is the exchange of labor for compensation.

The capitalist class is, however, not exchanging their labor. In the past, capitalism drove innovation and met growing demand. Now, money and labor are stolen through the exploitation of people who simply don't know any better. An agenda is pushed daily through the screens of every young person who owns an electronic device, enticing them to buy more, accumulate more, and fill the void of social belonging taken from them by the very device advertising is streamed through.

The situation goes beyond merely keeping us uneducated, though. Wages are being cut, and certain industries have experienced more layoffs than ever before in history. The very mechanism that keeps capitalism afloat—consumers—is being squeezed from every angle. Why?

In 2023, the US saw a surge in union-orchestrated strikes (Graduate Center & Office of Communications and Marketing, 2023). Across the globe, labor actions rippled in almost every capitalist economy with workers rising against benefit reductions and unsustainable wage increases (if any at all).

The working class is demanding education. They insist on the knowledge required to *know* what to do with their money and expect to be compensated for their part in driving the capitalist system. Without education, those who are not wealthy are more susceptible to being sold the pipe dream that money is meant to be spent frivolously.

We're losing money, hundreds of thousands of dollars at a time, all because we are not afforded the basic right of financial literacy. And it comes down to greed. Those who make the highest rate of profit win and it's harder to win when you're not cheating.

Some would argue that it's the capitalist system that promotes greed but I disagree. There is a place for capitalist economies. These economies work well when people are provided with the fundamental right to financial literacy education. The elite few don't want this. They want the wealth of many to be controlled and used by the few—much like a communist economy.

The Contributing Factors to Wealth Inequality

I'm by no means denying that there has always been some form of wealth inequality. Scholars of religious texts will tell you that wealth inequality was even present in biblical times, long before capitalist economies were established. Certain skills and a free market mean that some professions can trade at higher rates, while others will not.

Several factors can contribute to the gap in wealth widening, some personal choice, others completely out of our control and yet more require us to take control of our financial future. The top three of these factors are what truly stand out as changeable factors we *do* have control over if we're prepared to take matters into our own hands.

1. **Wages:** At the top of the inequality list is compensation for skills. In a true capitalist economy, the market price of a skill is determined by demand and supply. The more a skill is in demand, the higher the wage. Union strikes and uneven wage inflation in comparison to living costs show that other forces are at play, though. While the rapid expansion of technology certainly hasn't helped with wage inflation, one can't help but wonder if profiteering is the driving force behind relatively stagnant wages. The federal minimum wage in the US is still $7.25 per hour and the average cost of a very modest life is $10.40 per hour (Bloomenthal, 2022)—and that's assuming everyone is working eight hours per day.

2. **Education:** This is a big one. I'm not talking about different levels of education and the corresponding skills for fair compensation. The impact of basic financial education profoundly affects a person's ability to not only earn properly but to know what to do with their finances in general. In developing countries, where wealth inequality is disproportionately wide, living from hand to mouth is an everyday occurrence. People simply don't know how to properly plan for their financial future or how to budget for that matter. But the US is arguably not a developing country, is it? So, why does it have similar wealth inequality statistics to its less developed counterparts? Education, or more accurately, a lack of financial education. Added to this, in the US receiving the same level of education doesn't mean receiving the same quality of education. Different levels of funding affect the quality of education taught in the US and if we learned anything from the removal of Magill and Gay, the funders don't want financial literacy to be taught in *all* schools.

3. **Choice:** This is a tough one because I generally believe that we all have an innate ability to play a part in determining our wealth. The late Maya Angelou (2019) said, "Do the best you can until you know better. Then, when you know better, do better." The issue is that we need to *know* first. We need the foundational tools required to do *better* and those are not being supplied to our young adults. As parents, we need to ensure our children receive not just the education needed to make good financial decisions, but the *quality of* relevant information for their generation. What worked for us as Gen Xers doesn't work for our kids. We weren't faced with a constant bombardment of temptation. We weren't being forced into a dark room to navigate the landscape of financial health alone, and we certainly weren't taught that accumulation was the source of contentment and self-actualization. The capitalist dream we were sold was realistic, achievable even, but for our kids, it's a fever dream of accumulating things they don't want.

Financial Illiteracy and Its Consequences

One in five teens today can't create a simple budget (Choose FI Foundation, 2021), and this is only one of many other frightening statistics on various simple financial concepts that teenagers and young adults lack information on. A more dire realization when reading these statistics is that a lack of simple financial knowledge means teenagers and young adults know very little about any existing policies and laws imposed on markets to protect teenagers against fraud or any unfair plays.

Capitalism, at its core, involves personal interest, and the interest of corporations and many market players is to make profits. The one thing that most heavyweights of trade know is that many Americans lack general financial knowledge. Instead of focusing on improving their products to stay ahead of their competition and become innovative (one of the key characteristics of capitalism), they take advantage of a lack of financial literacy.

A combination of manipulation tactics in the media and the persistent sale of an American dream that no longer exists reinforces trade profiteering through what can only be described as unscrupulous means—when your elders say, "They don't make it like they used to," they're not lying.

In 2022, the National Financial Educators Council (NFEC) conducted a survey, asking American adults how much money they lost due to a lack of financial education. A little over 3,000 people responded, estimating an average loss of $1,819 each. Once this data was extrapolated to match the U.S. adult population, it was found that $436 billion was lost due to financial illiteracy. That is more money than the gross domestic profit of large developing countries (Stoll, 2023).

What Is Financial Illiteracy?

According to the NFEC, *financial illiteracy* is, "A lack of skills and knowledge on finance matters to confidently take effective action that best fulfills an individual's personal, family, and global community goals" (Field, 2019).

This is in stark contrast to the definition of *financial illiteracy* provided by the U.S. government, which is "not being able to reduce debt over time, pay bills promptly or even reconcile a bank account."

One definition is our ability to set financial goals for ourselves while the other implies we need to accrue debt and know how to pay this debt as well as our monthly costs. Many Americans are shocked when I tell them that several countries around the world do not require a person to have a credit card or take out loans to build their credit score. In fact, many first-world countries don't use credit scoring systems at all—creditworthiness is based on a person's ability to *afford* debt.

The systems in place, rampant consumerism, and a lack of financial knowledge set young Americans up to fail financially. They believe that they need to drown themselves in debt—to struggle financially—to be worthy of a credit score for larger life purchases or even so that they can receive a college education.

The Personal Cost of Financial Illiteracy

The above NFEC statistic aside, financial illiteracy comes at an exorbitant personal cost. On one end of the scale, not being financially secure in the future and retirement is one thing but the day-to-day bleeding of money is quite another.

Everything from fees and interest rates to financial yields on investments is affected by the level of financial knowledge acquired. Examining the minor physical costs of financial illiteracy may seem petty but this is part of the problem. On a fundamental level, the younger generation doesn't understand that the dollar lost compounds and the interest lost is the difference between financial freedom and constraint.

Minor costs that add up and could be negotiated or even controlled by the consumer are systemically rampant in the US. Bank, additional service, ATM withdrawal, and overdraft fees rob unsuspecting Americans of hundreds of dollars per month—and don't get me started on credit card interest and fees.

What all of this does is open up a can of worms. People become desperate to control their spending in a financial economy they don't know better. Over time, this pressure mounts, and desperation turns to fear as they realize they need to do something—anything to gain financial control. When fear increases, decision-making becomes poor, the possibility of identity theft and fraud rises, and even worse decisions are made in the form of debt that is not manageable in an already difficult economic climate.

The connection between capitalism and financial illiteracy is by no means a new phenomenon but the fact that our millennials are not contributing or investing in any of the retirement options available to them is startling. According to a study, 66% of Millennials aren't investing at all and have absolutely no savings outside of their short-term goals even if more than two-thirds of them work for a company that sponsors a retirement plan. Even more shockingly, only 5% of Millennials are actively saving for their retirement and statistics show that it all comes down to financial illiteracy (Brown, 2018).

There is no getting around it—a solid foundation in financial literacy is required if people are to avoid debt traps, low credit scores, and financial insecurity. The challenges faced by our Millennials and Gen Zers extend far beyond Gen X's lifespan and signal a cascade of perpetual poverty cycles as well as limited personal growth opportunities (Lach & Nzorubara, 2023).

Navigating Capitalism With Financial Literacy

Financial literacy is a tool that allows us to see through the smoke and mirror acts of unscrupulous capitalism. To understand this statement, it's important to examine the meaning and roots of the word capitalism.

"Capitalism" is derived from the word "capital," an evolved form of the word *caput* which means "head." Interestingly, it is also the origin of the words "chattel" and "cattle" (movable property). The -

ism is derived from the Latin word *isma* which signifies the practice of teaching something (Online Etymology Dictionary, n.d.). We can, therefore, presume that to thrive in a capitalist society, we must use our heads and educate ourselves and our children to become financially literate.

Financial literacy is a tool we use to see through the illusion created for us so that we can navigate capitalism without a consumer mindset. Money and business have a universal language that we need to become aware of if we are to survive the harsh realities of this new brand of capitalism. Failure to do so will result in us being robbed clean and being perpetually left behind in the next economic turns that are forthcoming. Let's make sure that we are not left behind by intensifying our financial education.

With a basic understanding of the nature of capitalism and how it is built on financial literacy, we can begin to untangle ourselves from the web of consumerism and define the role consumer behavior plays in perpetuating a greed-based capitalist economy. This begs the question: If financial illiteracy in a capitalistic environment is causing young people to fall into the effects of consumerism, what battles do we face to pull the same people out of it?

Personal Finance Highlights

1. Understanding Wealth Inequality in Capitalism: It's crucial to grasp the extent of wealth inequality in capitalist societies like the United States, where a small percentage of the population holds the majority of the wealth. This disparity is masked by metrics like GDP per capita, but recognizing it is essential for making informed financial decisions.

2. The Role of Financial Illiteracy: Financial illiteracy exacerbates the detrimental effects of capitalism on individuals, particularly teenagers and young adults. Lack of financial education leaves individuals vulnerable to exploitation by corporations, perpetuating a cycle of debt and financial insecurity.

3. Factors Contributing to Inequality: Wages, education, and personal choice are key factors contributing to wealth inequality. Stagnant wages, inadequate financial education, and societal pressures drive individuals into financial instability. Empowering individuals with financial literacy is crucial in addressing these factors.

4. Comparison with Other Economic Systems: Contrasting capitalism with socialist and communist economies reveals the unique challenges and consequences of each system. While capitalism offers opportunities for innovation and prosperity, unchecked wealth inequality and financial illiteracy can undermine its benefits.

5. The Power of Financial Literacy: Financial literacy serves as a tool for navigating the complexities of capitalism. By understanding the principles of finance and consumer behavior, individuals can make informed decisions and resist the allure of consumerism. Financial literacy empowers individuals to take control of their financial futures and challenge the status quo of capitalism's exploitative practices.

6. Capitalism is a system of trading where individuals operate to serve their interests and needs with little to no interference from the government.

7. With Capitalism and inequality, for every $1.7 million dollars the super-wealthy makes, regular folks make $1.

8. Financial illiteracy is, "A lack of skills and knowledge on finance matters to confidently take effective action that

best fulfills an individual's personal, family, and global community goals.

9. A solid foundation in financial literacy is required if people are to avoid debt traps, low credit scores, and financial insecurity.

10. To thrive in a capitalist society, we must use our heads and educate ourselves and our children to become financially literate.

CHAPTER 3
THE BATTLE AGAINST CONSUMERISM

E xperian's 2024 credit report showed that the average consumer debt for young adults between 18 and 24 is an astounding $10,942 (Horymski, 2024). More shockingly, this debt does not include mortgage debts.

The lessons we can learn about consumerism and how this system works can help us form an adequate defense system. By defending ourselves and our children from the ruthless tactics of consumerism, we begin to understand the value of defining financial success and are consequently less likely to fall into consumer traps.

Jeff Bezos is quoted as saying, "What consumerism really is, at its worst is getting people to buy things that don't actually improve their lives." Consumer culture is most often cultivated because of the greed involved in the profiteering aspects of capitalism. This greed is the driving force behind the consumer-to-consumer competition—keeping up with the Jones or the FOMO—we see. It is also the single most common cause behind the mindset that accumulation will somehow fill emotional and psychological voids or that our identity is somehow wrapped up in what we own rather than who we are.

The Consumer Trap

As we now know, capitalism is only possible because of supply and demand. The more demand for a certain product there is, the higher the supply needs to become to meet the demand for a product—and we're talking about true capitalism here. When demand for a product is consistently low, suppliers should theoretically take this as the first sign to begin market research. Once the supplier knows what the consumer needs to solve their problems, they can innovate and improve so that *real* solutions are put out into the marketplace.

All of this takes time and effort on the part of the producer but in a true capitalist economy, this doesn't matter because market research, ideation, and product iteration are ongoing. This, however, is not happening in the United States because the system is being cheated for a much easier, quicker solution that costs producers less time and effort, resulting in higher profits: consumerism.

I have never been a big fan of Valentine's Day. In my opinion, this is consumerism's biggest stage of the year for absolute wasteful spending. Let me break it down: Christmas is high on the list, but it does promote family bonding along with celebrating Jesus Christ's birthday. Valentine's, however, is a force for foolish spending.

Now, I love Lindt Chocolate Truffles! Society says that they make the perfect Valentine's Day gift. However, I eat these chocolates all year long. In this one store, they have these grand displays to convince you to purchase a $30 package of Lindt's for your special someone. The more money spent, the more special the gift.

I noticed that one 8.5-ounce bag of Lindt White Chocolate Candy Truffles costs $7.82. However, as Valentine's Day approaches, the demand is higher and the new display of Lindt chocolates is now $9.99! But once Valentine's Day is over, on February 15th, the demand drops and the price for those same chocolate truffles is now $3.99! Consumerism forces us to buy those truffles at $9.99, whereas if we wait one more day, the cost is $3.99, while supplies last! I have 365 days to express my love for someone. Why is that one day so important versus all the other 364 days?

The mechanisms of a consumerism-driven economy are nothing short of psychological warfare. Ruthless marketing tactics designed to manifest an insatiable appetite for material possessions, regardless of the quality, are the driving force behind rampant consumerism. Often, no forethought is given to cost, functionality, or needs-driven purchases, with consumerism honing in on the illusion that we can't possibly belong because of who we are.

Our young adults have been bombarded by this psychological warfare since they first laid hands on a digital device. They've been taught that their value is not wrapped up in experiences but in possessions, and worse yet, they lack the financial literacy and wear with all to withstand the onslaught they're facing.

Marketing tactics have shifted from solving consumer problems and needs to peer pressure and outright bullying tactics. More and more people are buying sub-quality products in the hope of peer validation and social proof. Don't believe me? Corporations have spent millions on developing algorithms that entice us to buy "value-added" items based solely on what other people have bought. Trend chasing as a result of social media depictions of perfectly balanced lives, hustle culture, unqualified reviews, and the FOMO have all replaced quality production. In essence, corporations have found a cheaper, more effective way to compel people to buy.

Brand alignments further drive accumulation with exclusivity being advertised as a temptation to spend more. If you want to watch a variety of newly released films or a series, you better be prepared to have multiple streaming subscriptions. If you decide to resist the temptation, you'll be bombarded by social media reviews from people you know or think you know, endless celebrity punts, and offers of "free" trial periods. All of this is designed to force a purchase based on nothing other than the need to belong to a social group that has what you want but doesn't necessarily need.

Consumerism and Teenagers

In the US, teens capture $44 billion in buying power (Wertz, 2018). What we must understand, however, is that our Millennials and Gen Zers are either no longer teens or are in the latter phases of their teen years. Gen Zs born closer to the Alpha cusp, and Gen Alphas, are proving to be less susceptible to consumerism tactics. While no adequate studies have been done into why this is occurring, the consensus is that these later generations have become desensitized to social media (Madison, 2021). I would argue this isn't a good thing either, because it compels consumer-driven practices to become more manipulative with their tactics.

Presently, Millennials hold the largest percentage of buying power in the US. Gen Zs are not far off, vying for first place. Combined, these two generations spanning 19 years, command a whopping 52.3% of all purchases made. We need to pay attention to this statistic because Gen Z also holds the dubious first-place position for racking up the highest credit card debt in a year, with Millennials holding the second-highest increase in debt (Wagatha & Chen, 2023). Of course, Gen Xers still hold the largest total capital debt but this makes sense as it includes mortgages and large asset purchases.

Studies done on hybrid capitalist-consumerism economies show that the effects of materialistic value on young minds are devastating. Low self-esteem, depression, and lowered purchase satisfaction point to increases in everything from mental health issues to a lack of empathy, lowered intrinsic values, reduced academic performance, and even increased substance abuse (Kaur & Kaur, 2016).

A lack of confidence not only in themselves but in financial knowledge means our young adults are more susceptible to consumerism tactics and instant gratification because our youth aren't taught the value of setting financial goals coupled with a burning desire to fit in fuels consumerism. Young adults simply don't understand the consequences of their actions now or in their precarious future and it's up to us to give them the tools they need to successfully overcome consumerism.

The Financial Consequences of Unchecked Consumerism

I'll begin by saying that any way we look at it, consumerism is designed with the view that the consumer is a cash cow. The sole goal of organizations deploying consumerism tactics is to increase consumption for the benefit of an organization's profits and not for the economy as a whole.

True capitalism is designed to balance consumer trends, creating planned obsolescence of certain consumer goods. This not only encourages companies to make more long-lasting, quality products, but it also forces marketing and advertising executives to become focused on targeting consumer needs rather than wants.

An equilibrium in consumer consumption ensures that the economy remains balanced on the spectrum of too much saving and too much spending. There is a direct correlation between increased costs of living and consumption and often, the conspicuous nature of consumerism drives a wasteful negative-sum activity in an already sensitive economic environment. This means consumers waste otherwise needed resources that are used to produce goods that hold no value or use, purely for the sake of the image they portray. This phenomenon is known as conspicuous consumption and imposes an enormous threat on the consumer and the entire economy.

While consumerism is often criticized in studies on sociological, environmental, and psychological grounds, we cannot ignore the financial implications of this type of spending. To keep up with trends, and to sustain a bottomless pit of wants, consumers often get themselves into unmanageable debt. The urge to spend is not ever mindfully weighed against the rising cost of living, and for those who are financially illiterate, the concept of "the bill always comes due" is lost.

The sudden realization that we're drowning in debt most often comes too late, and worse, our youth lack the knowledge to know how to dig themselves out of debt while still saving for a comfortable future. Feelings of hopelessness and resignation at the fact that they will be paying for their purchases for the remainder of their lives set in, and they don't realize they don't need to perpetuate the consumer cycle.

The American capitalist system is rigged—it's biased in favor of a seven percent-driven society that generates conspicuous consumerism. If we were to educate our youth, we'd eliminate this system bias. In highlighting the importance of mindful consumption, we hand back control to our younger generations and allow them to live a life where they prioritize their needs over their wants and reduce excess consumption. We allow them the opportunity to make informed decisions about their purchases and teach them the resilience they require to delay purchases that are of no worth to them outside of external validation. Most importantly, we begin to tip the scales of financial inequality to a more balanced position where the majority are in control of their finances.

The Mindful Consumer

With all that has been explained about the system's nature and how it is designed to leach present and future money from us, it becomes more apparent why we need to take steps to protect our financial health.

Effective use of money is one thing, but this only comes with education and experience, and we need to find ways to overcome the psychological warfare happening in the present. I'm not a proponent of doing all things at once, and for good reason. Looking at the bigger picture gives us an indication of what an outcome is but it can also be very overwhelming trying to figure out how to achieve this outcome.

James Clear (2018), the author of *Atomic Habits*, discusses the benefits of the one-percent rule. Under this rule, the goal is not to try to change everything that is going wrong but to improve in minuscule amounts until a desired outcome is reached.

When it comes to the consumer onslaught, the one percent rule can be applied in the form of mindful consumption—a practice that requires us to become aware of what we're spending and whether or not we *need* to make a purchase.

Of course, mindful consumption and spending require knowledge and effort on our behalf, as well as introspection so that we can identify what our spending triggers are and what consumerism tactics are being used to entice us. Once we can identify *why* we're spending and *what* we're unnecessarily spending on, it becomes far easier to take control of our finances. It allows us to align our spending with our financial goals and values with the future financial outcomes we have set for ourselves. The simplified steps to mindful spending and consumption are as follows:

- Establish your goals and values when it comes to financial freedom—remember, your definition of success and financial freedom is not necessarily the same as others. I've spoken to many people who, after becoming introspective, realized that flashy cars and a large house went completely against what they wanted. And by subscribing to consumerism, they were moving further away from their financial goals.
- Break down your financial goals into one-percent steps— decide what is easiest to let go of when it comes to spending habits and ditch these first.
- Next, you're going to need to set up self-discipline safety nets. Discuss daily withdrawal and spending limits with your financial institution, cut up credit cards, and make a commitment to your future self that you will work in the present to ensure financial security. Remember, the decisions you make at 20 are the ones you will have to live with when you're 50!
- Make a list of your spending triggers and habits and place this list everywhere—and I do mean everywhere. Make it the background of your phone, laptop, and tablet. Have written lists next to your common online spending areas, and keep the list in your wallet next to your most used

cards. This will remind you to be mindful when spending and will interrupt the habit loop you're stuck in.

- When the urge to spend is too strong, give yourself a cool-off period. Take 24 hours to think about the purchase, create a list of pros and cons, and be mindful of whether or not you're *convincing* yourself that you *need* something rather than wanting it. Go online, look up negative customer reviews, and ignore positive reviews (these are often sponsored or paid-for reviewers).
- Create a vision board of what your future looks like and put it somewhere you can see it often. Make sure to list the benefits of mindful spending in the present on this board.
- Finally, learn the art of turning the FOMO into the joy of missing out (JOMO). This might sound ridiculous to you now, but learning the JOMO will assist in redirecting your attention to the present. When you can begin to appreciate the value of not accumulating things that don't serve you, you can turn jealousy and resentment into a deep contentment that others will sometimes have that you don't have.

The Benefits of Mindful Spending

Goals are more easily pursued when we have a reason for changing our behaviors. Highlighting the benefits of mindful consumption provides us with a robust foundation on which we can build a list of benefits that are meaningful to us. In addition, it allows us to identify not only our financial needs but our psychological needs too. This helps to build a future that is less reliant on external validation and more centered around creating a life that is relevant to us as individuals.

Before reading the benefits below, I'd like to highlight that there is nothing wrong with wanting material goods. If the latest gadgets, cars, or designer wear are important to you, then you should focus your attention on how to purchase these things without going into unmanageable debt. Mindful consumption is about finding a balance and knowing that you are in control of your purchase and your financial future.

1. **Financial independence:** Perhaps the most critical benefit to mindful consumption is becoming independent. When you know how to budget, prioritize your needs over your wants, and pursue financial goals, you're more likely to become independent over time.

2. **Understanding the value of savings:** I get it, the last thing you're thinking of right now is old age because you have plenty of other large life milestones to achieve before retirement. But going to college, buying a car, traveling, purchasing a home, all of these milestones require careful planning to ensure you're not drowning in debt.

3. **Honoring yourself:** Peer pressure when combined with consumerism pressure can be overwhelming. Mindful consumption and understanding that what we purchase doesn't define us helps ease the anxiety created by external pressure and has us living a life that is aligned with our goals and values. There are a lot of very wealthy people out there who live a frugal life while enticing you to buy so don't be fooled into thinking that wealth and possessions are mutually inclusive.

A Word on Minimalism

Minimalism was trendy for a while before it was subject to smear campaigns. One can only presume that these campaigns were instigated by the consumerism powers that be to devalue a science-backed practice.

Studies show that the wealthiest (and happiest) countries around the globe practice minimal consumption and embrace a minimalist life. Living a life that is minimalist means valuing and prioritizing rich experiences over owning possessions. Lifestyle and what is bought are focused on quality and not quantity. This means minimalists still own property but they exercise their right to buy this property because of its value, not its status. Consequently, these countries have far greater wealth equality and dramatically lower rates of depression and anxiety (Malik & Ishaq, 2023).

The principles of minimalism are simple:

- **Less is more:** Minimalism encourages the idea that having fewer possessions can lead to financial freedom and reduced stress. Teenagers can benefit from the understanding that accumulating too many material possessions can strain their finances over time and lower happiness.
- **Prioritizing value:** Minimalism encourages individuals to focus on what truly adds value to their lives. Teenagers can apply this principle by being selective about their spending and investing in items or experiences that align with their values and long-term goals.
- **Reducing debt and increasing savings:** Minimalism's emphasis on simplicity and frugality can help teenagers avoid unnecessary debt and build healthy savings habits. By avoiding excessive consumerism and living within their means, they can allocate more of their income toward savings and investments.

The Anti-Consumerism Toolkit

To confront consumerism head-on, we need to build a toolkit that protects our mental health as well as our financial well-being in the present and the future.

Each of the tools listed below will be expanded upon in future chapters, assisting you in managing your money through each of the phases of your young adult life. Before reading the information below, you must know that some aspects of future chapters may be known to you, and others may have been overlooked in the limited financial education you've received. As such, I strongly encourage you to read through each chapter so that you have a wealth of knowledge to build your financial future.

With that aside, let's take a look at some of the tools you need to counteract consumerism tactics.

- Learn how to budget and track your expenses.
- Develop good shopping habits. Create meal plans, have shopping lists, and be mindful about priority purchases.
- Take the time to set short-, mid-, and long-term financial goals for yourself. Break each of these goals down into one-percent milestones you can achieve.
- Remove the stigma of using coupons and discounts to your advantage. One dollar saved on ten items is ten dollars saved!
- Limit online buying where possible and ignore the "Others who have bought this also like this" suggestions. What other people own is not what you should own. The movie *The Social Network* is a powerful reminder that "the consumer has become the product!" (Fincher, 2010).
- Practice mindfulness when deciding on purchases and institute 24-hour cool-off periods often.

- Get comfortable with comparative shopping. Often, certain items are discounted or simply cheaper at different stores.
- Become a pro at dealing with peer pressure and the need for external validation—turn the FOMO into the JOMO for a healthier financial and mental well-being future.
- Choose to control the things you can control when it comes to your finances. This includes your spending habits, the "needs" purchases you make, and saving and investing.
- Become marketing savvy. Look into marketing trends, uncover the exploitive tactics being used, and remain open-minded to the fact that you're probably being manipulated into a purchase. This will ensure you're not hitting "buy" and regretting it later.

It's important to acknowledge that the financial literacy gap in our education system is intentional. A combination of rampant consumerism and capitalist greed has created an environment in which our young adults are navigating treacherous terrain without a roadmap.

Advocating for financial literacy is important, but the wheels of bureaucracy turn slowly, especially when the cogs are controlled by the wealthy 7%. The only way to ensure we have the knowledge we need for a secure financial future is to educate ourselves and make the conscious decision to not fall into the same traps as the majority of the 93%. Now that we have identified why teens and young adults need to achieve financial literacy, let's see if we can identify the basics of obtaining financial literacy.

Personal Finance Highlights

At the culmination of this eye-opening chapter on consumerism and its impact on our financial well-being, it's imperative to distill the key takeaways that empower us to navigate the treacherous waters of consumer culture.

1. Understanding the Financial Landscape: Experian's 2024 credit report sheds light on the staggering average consumer debt among young adults, underscoring the urgent need for financial literacy. This knowledge arms us with the awareness to recognize and resist the relentless pressures of consumerism, thereby safeguarding our financial future.
2. Unveiling the Consumer Trap: Through vivid anecdotes and insightful analysis, the chapter exposes the mechanisms of a consumerism-driven economy as a form of psychological warfare. From inflated prices on Valentine's Day chocolates to the manipulation of social media algorithms, readers are urged to recognize and resist the tactics employed by corporations to perpetuate excessive consumption.
3. Empowering Youth with Financial Literacy: The chapter underscores the importance of equipping young adults with the knowledge and skills necessary to navigate the complexities of personal finance in a consumer-driven society. By addressing the lack of financial literacy among youth and providing practical strategies for mindful spending and saving, individuals can empower themselves to make informed financial decisions and resist the allure of consumerism.
4. Embracing Mindful Consumption: Highlighting the benefits of adopting a mindset of mindful consumption,

the chapter encourages readers to reevaluate their spending habits and prioritize financial goals aligned with their values. By embracing minimalism and prioritizing experiences over possessions, individuals can cultivate financial independence, reduce debt, and enhance overall well-being.

5. Building Your Anti-Consumerism Toolkit: Concluding with a practical toolkit for countering consumerism, the chapter equips readers with actionable strategies to take control of their finances and resist the pressures of excessive consumption. From budgeting and goal-setting to practicing mindfulness and savvy shopping habits, individuals are empowered to reclaim agency over their financial futures and break free from the cycle of consumerism.

PART TWO
BUILDING A STRONG FINANCIAL EDUCATION (AGES 15-18)

When life has you bewildered,
"JUMP INTO THE POOL!"
That forces us to think in a new direction.
And when you get out of the pool, **FORECAST** *it out!*

CHAPTER 4
FINANCIAL LITERACY
101 FOR TEENS

W hat if we viewed money not just as a way to buy things, but as a tool to shape the kind of life we want to lead? How would our spending habits and financial decisions change?

Between the ages of 15 and 18, we begin to become curious about independence. We may prepare to purchase our first car, start thinking about further education paths, and dream about a life in our own space. We love our parents and take their financial cover for granted, but our responsibility and decision-making quotients are gaining momentum, and we want to move away from our parents' oversight. Becoming independent, however, is very difficult without financial literacy or knowing what it means to be financially literate.

What Is Financial Literacy

"Financial literacy" is the knowledge required to understand several different financial concepts. These range from the basics of budgeting and saving to more advanced techniques like healthy debt management, investments, taxes, and compound interest.

With financial literacy, we can analyze our past money habits, apply changes in these habits to the present, and properly plan and work toward a healthy financial future with good money habits. In other words, financial literacy is the tool we use to make informed, responsible financial decisions for ourselves.

Without financial literacy, we're navigating dark and treacherous waters with no direction, no compass, and no destination in mind —we're hoping for the best but have no idea what the worst outcome could be!

You may be wondering, *Why does all of this matter at your age?* You have your adult guardians or parents as a safety net right now, so surely what you do with your money now doesn't matter!

Allow me to ask some questions. Did your parents tell you about the struggle to get you potty trained? Perhaps you remember the struggle of learning how to tie your shoelaces? Can you use the restroom and tie your shoelaces now without a struggle?

The actions and behaviors we learn when we are younger through repetition and reward are what form the habits we have today, and that is why learning financial literacy in young adulthood is important. The financial habits we form today are the financial habits that will carry us through our entire adulthood and will be the single most powerful tool we have against consumerism and greed-based capitalism. Let's break down the other benefits of early financial literacy development:

- **Developing early financial habits:** These financial habits will have us set for life and we won't have to struggle to learn them later in our lives. Making sound financial decisions will become an automatic response throughout our adult lives.

- **Becoming independent and responsible:** Financial literacy eases our transition into adulthood. We will already know what we *need* to live a comfortable life (rent, balanced nutritional food, and transportation) and will know how to manage our *want* spending urges.
- **Avoiding debt and pitfalls:** We will know what debt traps are out there and have the confidence to avoid unnecessary costs, negotiate rates and fees, and set healthy financial boundaries for ourselves.
- **Setting and achieving financial goals:** We can set financial goals that align with our values and purpose in life and more importantly, know how to set and achieve milestones for success. This reduces the anxiety we can feel when making big-ticket purchases, like buying a home, because we know that we can manage our finances and have safety nets in place.
- **Investing for the future:** We begin to understand the value of saving for the future and know what these savings mean. We know that investment goes beyond just stashing away cash and know how to make our money work for us —even when we're sleeping.

Financial literacy helps us to develop the skills we need to build a financially secure future and to follow our passions in life without the stress and anxiety of owing a whole lot of money to capitalist organizations. We can begin to unravel the web of lies we've been taught about social belonging and *consensually* part ways with the money we have earned in return for the property we *need* both in the present and our future.

Money Basics

A lot of us believe that money is the cash and coins we have in our hands or the cards we swipe or tap. I bet a couple of us still remember a time when we thought money was never-ending—when we couldn't understand why the adults in our lives couldn't just insert their cards into an ATM and a machine would dispense a stream of cash like an unlimited Pez dispenser.

Now, what if I told you that money is not never-ending? What if I said that the amount of money circulating in the US is finite and that the treasury printing more money is a *very, very,* bad sign for the economy?

Money is like any other product in the capitalist marketplace. For it to hold its value or have a good value, the supply needs to be balanced. To understand what money is, we need a quick history lesson.

Back before printers or even written text, people would trade one skill for another. If you had a farm with dairy cows, you would trade milk or even a dairy cow with another farmer for something you needed like eggs or a chicken.

As time went on, people discovered that others wanted physical property that was rare or difficult to find. This property was everything from seashells to animals and gold, silver, or precious stones. The more difficult the physical property was to find or obtain, the more value it held. This was the beginning of what we call commodity trading.

Having a whole lot of different commodities being traded was difficult though—imagine dragging around gold bars to buy a gallon of milk! So, people created coins made of gold or silver, and each coin had an assigned value. These were called fiat currencies and needed to have a commodity value attached to them.

Fast forward to today, when governments and private individuals own commodities. Instead of physically storing commodities, fiat currency (paper, coin, and digital money) is produced to represent the value of the commodity that backs it.

Back to the question of "What is money?" Money is the tool we use to trade for goods and services. When we earn money, we trade our time, capabilities, and knowledge for a commodity, which we then use to trade for someone else's time, capabilities, and knowledge. Fiat currency is required for common transactions, although some people still engage in bartering one service or good for another.

When it comes to money, you must understand that it yields enormous power but you can harness that power. *The consumerist idea that we need to earn money to spend it means your money has control over you*! For you to harness the power of money, you need to let go of the notion that money is the ultimate goal because it's not. It's simply the tool we use to achieve our goals.

Types of Income

With a solid understanding of money, we can now look at how we can earn money to achieve our goals.

- **Earned Income:** This is the most common form of income. It is earned when we exchange our skills or goods for currency. For example, working a part-time job packing shelves for a company would be the exchange of fiat currency for labor and time.
- **Passive income:** Income that is earned after an initial money or skills outlay and that continues to generate

money with minimal or no work is called passive income. Passive income can be in the form of income-earning assets, artistic licenses from producing books, online courses, music, and so on, or self-running business models, like programs that are created and used by others for a subscription fee.

- **Portfolio income:** This is money received from having monetary assets—I'll explain this a little later when we discuss investments.

There is one other form of income in the form of inheritance, prizes, and awards received. These are not planned for incomes and are nice to have but we have no control over whether we will receive money in this form or not.

It is common to mistake money that comes from debt as earned income. Debt income may serve the same purpose as earned income in that we can use it to purchase goods. However, debt money comes at a price. It has to be paid back with more money than we would have spent in the present moment—I will explain a bit more later in this chapter.

The Budgeting Blueprint

When it comes to a budget, "84% of Americans have a monthly budget but still overspend," (Marder, 2023). This statistic tells us exactly how influenced we are by consumerism! That's more than 260 million people between the ages of 15 and 69 who are spending more money than they intend to because of consumerism.

Learning how to budget and become resilient against consumerism tactics early on helps us avoid consumerism traps and build a financially secure future for ourselves. The easiest, and most effective way to learn how to budget is to begin with the 50-30-20 method—let's break it down:

- **50% of income:** Should be spent on our needs (rent, food, transport, basic clothing, education, utilities, insurance, and so on).
- **30% of income:** Should be spent on our wants (subscriptions, gym memberships, entertainment, streaming, designer clothing, and so on.)
- **20% of income:** Should go to saving and investments.

For the 50-30-20 method to work, we need to understand that everyone's needs are different. Someone who is working toward a scholarship based on academics will have very different needs than someone who has a scholarship based on sports, particularly a Division I scholarship. To maintain a sports scholarship, a gym membership is mandatory, whereas an academic scholarship may require extra tutoring and college prep courses.

Added to this, if we're going to budget well and not fall into the consumer trap, we need to be able to delay our wants spending so that we can build financial resilience. Sometimes this means flipping the 20% and 30% sections of this budgeting method around—30% to savings and investments and 20% to wants or allocating more of our 30% wants to our 50% needs budget.

What is important to remember when budgeting is that needs, savings, and investments take priority over wants. This doesn't mean depriving ourselves of our wants—simply that we may need to wait for what we want from time to time.

Savings and Investing Essentials

I remember attending a conference in Atlanta, GA, called "Secrets of a Millionaire Mind," which had about 1,600 people in attendance. An exercise was introduced during the conference where we had to divide into four mental money groups. At this time, I was only aware of two groups: savers and spenders. The fact that there were four was a very interesting discovery. The exercise required each person to identify which group they thought they belonged to and divide into four equal sections in accordance with the number of groups. I was part of the savers. The organizer called on us to identify the four equal sections and we did so with ease. Then the organizers called on the spenders to identify their four equal sections. The groups announced themselves all over the room and they were not equal in number at all between the groups. I was amazed by the amount of disorganization among the spenders—it said a lot about how different the two groups approached life, let alone money.

The Power of Saving

Saving has an ordered routine that leads to an organized outcome. Savers carefully consider the impact of decisions not just in money matters, but also in other areas of life. Adopting a saver mindset, however, doesn't happen overnight. We need to begin instituting one percent changes early on so that we can build our saving habits.

1. **Be consistent.** Start saving with your next paycheck! Decide on the percentage you will put away and take action. Remember, to become disciplined and to form a habit, you need to start somewhere, so commit, take action, and repeat every time you get paid. If you're not sure where to place your savings, you may want to use a

money market account which has a minimum account balance and limits the number of withdrawals you can make per month. It also helps you minimize risk to grow your savings with compound interest. Alternatively, begin with a regular savings account with no access (card). This will add an extra layer of security as you build discipline.

2. **Invest in your future.** Take a look at your vision board. What will you need financially to achieve the dreams you've recorded on your board? Saving is not just about stashing money away—it's also about making your money work for you. Consider investing a portion of your savings in assets like stocks, bonds, or mutual funds to potentially earn higher returns over the long term.

3. **Set clear goals.** Define what you're saving for. Whether it's a new phone, a trip, college, or something else, having specific goals makes saving more motivating. Break down your goals into smaller, manageable targets to track your progress.

4. **Budget wisely.** Create a budget to manage your income and expenses. This will help you consistently allocate a portion of your money toward savings. Knowing where your money goes allows you to make informed decisions about what you can save.

An Introduction to Investing

Investing is the art of spending money to have it grow. When you buy something that has no value, will decrease in value, or is designed to be used and replaced, your money will not grow—it will decrease. When you invest, however, your money is given the *chance* to multiply. For younger investors, like yourself, the investment methods below are an option. Keep in mind that banking and investing under the age of 18 will require a trustworthy, responsible adult to accompany and cosign with you.

- **Buying individual stocks:** Putting money into a listed company in exchange for fractional ownership of the company is buying stocks. When investing in stocks, you're buying a *share* of the company but do not physically own a part of the organization you're investing in. A company's growth and value, however, will increase your initial investment and the opposite happens when a company undergoes financial struggles or obstacles. Stock investors buy shares when the price is low and sell shares for a profit when the price is high.
- **Mutual funds:** Mutual funds are managed by professional investors who spread your money across different investment options. Mutual funds are great for young investors because you have a professional doing all of the work and research for you. These professionals are paid for their services through the commission and fees due when you invest.
- **Money market and high-yield savings accounts:** Traditional savings accounts are great but often don't grow your money by much. A two-percent interest-bearing savings account will double your money in 72 years! There are, however, high-yield savings and money market accounts that will provide you with way more bang for your buck and will double your money a whole lot faster.

There is no reason why you shouldn't begin investing and saving between the ages of 15 and 18 and while your options are limited, you *do* have options. At this stage of your financial literacy journey, your focus should be on low and no-risk investments, saving, and becoming disciplined with your budget so that you can stay out of debt and build a great credit record.

Understanding Credit

Did you know that young people aged 28 to 29 had an average debt of $12,871 in 2022 (Fay, 2023)?

One year, I had a group of sophomores from MIT that participated in my online money management course. In gaining feedback from them, one of the key factors that came out of it was their lack of knowledge associated with credit cards. Some of the students had already become victims of the "Turn 18, Eligible for a Credit Card" bum rush by credit card companies, thinking they were being offered free money. Some of the students refused to touch a credit card fearing the rumors associated with them. Do not believe the hype that credit cards represent free money. You can find yourself still paying off those credit balances 30 years later! However, credit cards, if used correctly, can become a tremendous asset in helping plan your financial future. As a result, I wrote a short pamphlet titled, *The Credit Choice: 10 Effective Ways to Use Credit Cards Without Incurring Major Debt,* which is available on Amazon for more details.

What Is Credit?

Credit is money received by individuals that is not regarded as income. This money is not taxed but is certainly not for free. You will need to pay back the money you have received when using credit plus extra in the form of interest and fees. The financial system integrated the credit system as a way of making a profit. There are different forms of credit, some easier to obtain and harder to pay off, and some harder to obtain but easier to pay off.

How much money you have loaned in the form of credit and how well you pay back the money you owe will affect your ability to purchase on credit in the future, whether or not you qualify for a rental, and even if you are eligible for certain jobs!

Building and Maintaining Good Credit

A credit score is a number given to a person that reflects how well they manage their money. This score is on a scale from 300 to 850. The lower your score, the more trouble you will have accessing credit, renting, and so on. You will also have to pay higher fees in the form of interest. Higher scores will mean you have more access to major loans like mortgages for asset purchases.

Your credit score will rise or fall based on your spending and repayment behaviors. The more regularly and responsibly you manage your income and any current debt you have, the better your credit score will become. You must know how to manage your debt and stay out of credit pitfalls (like revolving credit and credit) cards so that you can build and maintain a good credit score.

Debt Management Strategies

Debt is the money you owe to other people when you take credit. Ensuring you manage your debt properly will go a long way toward you becoming financially secure. The money you're lent in the form of credit needs to be paid back with fees and interest.

There are a few different types of debt, these include

- **Secured debt:** A loan that is taken out against an asset like a house or other property is called a secured debt. This physical property is used as insurance that you will pay your loan back and is called "collateral." If you don't pay your monthly installments on this type of debt, it will result in the lending institution taking back the item you purchased and selling it to someone else so they can get their money back.

- **Unsecured debt:** A loan that is taken out with *no* collateral is called an unsecured loan. These types of loans are offered based on your credit history and credit score. Medical bills, student loans, store credit, and so on are examples of unsecured debt.
- **Revolving debt:** This is also called an open line of credit. Unlike other forms of credit, you only stop having access to the credit amount once you reach the limit. For example, you may have $1,000 in credit, spend $200, and would still have access to $800. Payments to revolving debt will reduce a small amount of your initial loan amount. While revolving credit is tempting, it is notoriously difficult to pay off and requires a lot of discipline and knowledge to pay off the full balance owed. Credit cards are the most common form of revolving debt in the US.

- ○ Rule number one when it comes to debt is: If you can't afford it, don't buy it.
- ○ Rule number two is to understand how interest and fees work when it comes to paying back debt. Minimum required payments will always favor the interest amount over the capital amount, which means you're paying off fees rather than what you loaned for a long time.
- ○ Rule number three applies only to revolving debt. This rule is very important if you're going to use your credit card responsibly, so take note—If you cannot

pay the full balance in three monthly installments and *not* take any additional cash from your savings, investment, and needs spending, then you shouldn't use your credit card. Most people get into trouble with their credit cards because they're not thinking ahead. Do yourself the favor of saving yourself from debt stress and make use of this type of debt wisely.

Planning for Your Future Goals

At this point, you should have gained a bit of confidence when it comes to money. Financial plans have now become more than an abstract dream you don't know how to reach. But dreams aren't goals—they're simply the inspiration behind our goals and if we're going to achieve what we've envisioned for our financial future, we need to plan effectively.

Let's begin this planning with some questions:

- What do you think your current credit score or credit history is right now?
- What have you learned about your spending habits?
- What external influences that may affect you going over your budget are unique to you?
- What is your income situation like?

The answers to these questions will help you to see the gap between where you are in your financial journey now and where you are aiming to be in the future. The information you glean from analyzing your spending habits and what influences you will also allow you to use specific tools to help shield you against consumerism tactics.

When setting financial goals, they must be specific, measurable, achievable, realistic, and time-bound (SMART). This means committing to small, actionable steps you can take when it comes to your money that are not only relevant to you but achievable. A great way to do this without comparing yourself to others is to use the 50-30-20 method we talked about earlier and decide what percentages apply to you specifically.

Financial Safety Nets

Even with the best plans in place, life can sometimes happen. Accidents, illnesses, or other events outside of our control can set us back financially and impact the trajectory of our financial goals. While we cannot know when these bumps in the road will happen, certain safety nets can be anchored in place to help weather financial storms.

These safety nets come in different forms including saving for emergencies and insurance. Think of insurance as temporary financial compensation for incidences beyond our control. Now, insurance doesn't cover everything that could go wrong but for the big stuff, like a car accident, there is cover. The main types of insurance include

- **Life insurance:** Financial compensation given to the beneficiaries of someone after death.
- **Home insurance:** Coverage against loss of property (building structure and all inside things like furniture, appliances, and so on) due to fire, water, damage, theft, and some natural disasters.
- **Motor vehicle insurance:** Coverage for damages to your car due to collision or theft as well as third-party cover for pedestrians, property, or other vehicles involved in a crash.

- **Disability insurance:** Coverage against any loss of income due to inability to work after an accident.

There are other types of insurance, like travel, fraudulent card usage, and so on, and we must educate ourselves about what safety nets we can put in place for ourselves. Insurance is not free (nothing in life is), and we must understand that how much we pay is also dependent on our spending habits, credit score, age, and some other criteria like how many times an insurance policy has been claimed against.

Some forms of insurance are compulsory meaning they have to be taken out. Most often, compulsory insurance is included in loan amounts, like an auto loan or mortgage. Remember, anything bought on credit is not yours until the last payment is made and financial lending companies need to make sure the collateral they are financing is properly covered.

Wealth is built one step at a time. Proper saving, analysis of spending habits, choosing to live a life that prioritizes experiences over accumulating objects, and putting financial safety nets in place are all critical steps to creating financial freedom and meaningful wealth.

Building Resilience

Nelson Mandela (2019) said, "The greatest glory in living lies not in never failing, but in rising every time we fall."

Even with all the safety nets and planning in place, unexpected setbacks can happen. This is the nature of life and we need to be able to fortify ourselves against the inevitable setbacks that can occur. Building financial resilience helps us to think on our feet, tread water, and stay afloat when times are tough.

Of course, having a hefty savings plan in place helps, but what if we don't want to dip into our savings too much or simply haven't been saving long enough to keep us afloat financially?

Financial resilience teaches us that not many things in life are permanent and that we can learn from our mistakes and things outside of our financial control. At this age, we have a great safety net in our adult guardians, which means we should begin practicing the resilience-building steps below from a young age.

- Learn to manage your debt as early as possible and don't put yourself in unnecessary debt.
- Split your savings between future purchases and emergencies. This way, you won't need to dip into your "wants" savings when something unforeseen comes up. As time passes, when the unforeseen does show up, you have the flexibility to absorb it without detriment to your finances.
- Set financial goals, break them down into milestones, achieve them, and then set new goals. Continually challenging yourself to new financial heights will build your financial muscles just like going to the gym and eating healthy builds your body's muscles.
- Reward yourself for resilient behaviors. These don't need to be physical rewards, but rather, choose self-care or experience rewards.
- Finally, commit to learning from your mistakes. It's easy to throw your hands up in defeat, but learning from your mistakes and choosing not to make the same one twice is the best way to become financially resilient.

Learning From Others

Sixteen-year-old Emily landed a part-time job and was excited to earn her first paycheck. Like so many other young adults, she hadn't learned the value of saving money or setting financial goals and so she spent most of her earnings on entertainment, shopping, and dining out with friends. Financial emergencies or future goals didn't even cross Emily's mind until one day, her car broke down unexpectedly. With nothing saved to cover repair costs, Emily had to fall back on relying on her parents. The money borrowed to fix her car needed to be paid back and Emily learned a hard lesson about how limited life can be without savings and proper budgeting.

Determined to not repeat her mistake, Emily created a budget that included saving a portion of her income, creating an emergency fund, and setting financial goals for college and travel. With a proper budget in place, she was still able to enjoy her money, making the odd want purchase, going out from time to time, paying back her debt, and saving for her financial future.

What we can learn from Emily's experience is that if we are diligent in creating a budget that includes saving and investing in our future, we can still enjoy our lives without the stress of lurking unforeseen expenses.

With the information learned in this chapter, we can gain a deeper understanding of how money can be used to secure our financial future and that while money is meant to be spent, it's not meant for frivolous spending. With proper planning, saving, and investing, we can grow the money we make, achieve our financial dreams, and curate a credit score that unlocks the doors to meaningful purchases.

Personal Finance Highlights

1. Money as a Tool for Life Transformation: Imagine if we reframed our perspective on money, viewing it not merely as a means to acquire goods, but as a powerful tool to shape the life we desire. By embracing this mindset shift, we can make more intentional spending choices and financial decisions that align with our aspirations.

2. Empowerment Through Financial Literacy: Financial literacy is the cornerstone of making informed, responsible decisions about our finances. It empowers us to analyze past habits, make positive changes, and strategically plan for a secure financial future. Without this knowledge, we're adrift in uncertain waters, lacking direction and awareness of potential pitfalls.

3. Early Habits Shape Future Financial Well-being: Just as learning to tie our shoelaces or use the restroom became automatic behaviors through repetition, so too do our financial habits form in young adulthood. By developing sound financial habits early on, we set ourselves up for a lifetime of financial security and independence.

4. Budgeting: The Blueprint for Financial Resilience: Budgeting isn't about deprivation; it's about prioritization. By adopting the 50-30-20 method or a variation that suits our needs, we gain the ability to navigate consumerism traps, distinguish between needs and wants, and build a resilient financial future.

5. Credit and Debt Management: Keys to Financial Freedom: Understanding credit and debt is crucial for avoiding pitfalls that can hinder financial progress. By building and maintaining good credit, managing debt responsibly, and using credit cards wisely, we unlock opportunities for financial growth and security.

CHAPTER 5
THE POWER OF SAVING, INVESTING, AND COMPOUND INTEREST

C onversations about the state of the economy, highlighting the purpose of investing and saving, and admonition for frivolous spending when it comes to our teens are often the go-to "lesson plan." Our kids, however, have grown up somewhat different from us. Their world is less black or white and they live in an existence that is often so colorful that it causes them to overwhelm.

Added to this, kids do as we do and not as we say, so when we begin speaking about the limited opportunities available to us, financial uncertainty, or financial stress kids overhear and believe that their future is limited no matter how motivated, determined, or disciplined they are.

I am by no means saying we need to gloss over the realities of life but we do need to strike a balance where we provide our young adults with a direction and a reason why. This means limiting conversations that highlight financial struggles and providing them with the value of living a life that is financially responsible. A healthy money mindset is one that is balanced but *must* instill a sense of curiosity when it comes to valuable tools like saving, investing, and compound interest. We need to gear our conversations—intentional or overheard—to ones that embrace the lessons we have learned and the financial solutions available to us. We cannot instill this curiosity with fear.

Fear (false evidence appearing real): Consumerism is built around the illusion of fear. Fear that we won't belong unless we buy this specific thing. In the moment we are buying something, what are we not doing? Saving and investing. What happens when that fear is so deeply embedded within us, that we have a hard time functioning against it? I can attest to that. All of my life there was this thing that I was fighting from within that I had no idea what it was. I couldn't explain it and I couldn't define it. All I knew was it would show up in the most inopportune moments. When I was 28 years old, I was talking to my mother on the phone, and suddenly, she started telling me about this story when she was 12 years old.

One evening, her best friend told her that her mother's boyfriend molested her. The boyfriend told her that if she told anyone about it, he would kill her. The next morning, reports came that the police had found my mother's friend lying face down in a creek. As a 12-year-old, my mother blamed herself for the murder because she was the one her friend told. When my mother told me that story, I felt a massive shock shoot down my spine from head to toe! The fear my mother had from that incident had manifested itself in me. Fear of being an outsider. Fear of being in isolation. Fear is a real emotion, but we cannot allow it to give us a false sense of "Well I am broke anyway, so I might as well spend the little that I have." We must act in discipline despite our fears, especially when it comes to saving and investing.

One of the most profound lessons wealthy young adults are taught is to prepare for their financial future without catastrophizing it. Instead of living in a world of negative "what-ifs," they're provided with the right tools to confidently take financial risks that pay off. The reason for this is that these risks are well-thought-out and come with the safety net of investment and compound interest.

Unleashing the Power of Saving and Investing

Tony Robbins (2016) defines financial security as the ability to pay for the five basic financial needs in life—food, shelter, clothing, transportation, and insurance, with the interest that accumulates in our bank accounts.

Consumerism hones in on neglecting these five basic financial needs for our human need to belong and be accepted by society. Young adults are particularly susceptible to consumerism because social belonging is incredibly important while we are coming to terms with and discovering our independent identity away from the adults in our lives. As we struggle with who we are and what we will become, we look for the comfort and safety of a group.

Now, social belonging is a powerful need that is rooted in our biology and when we reach our teen years, the changes and development in our brains highlight this need—that's why we get FOMO so often! We don't want to miss out on what our friends are doing; we want safety from our guardians, but we're also trying to establish our unique identity, and it can be confusing!

Consumerism exploits us at a time when our identity is still forming. It feeds us the illusion that we can find a shortcut to who we are and find belonging by buying stuff. But consumerism is just that—nothing but an illusion—and we can only truly find our sense of identity in our independence and in the positive people we surround ourselves with. Ironically, this independence is often delayed because of consumerism—its impact on excess spending and debt means we cannot afford to move out of our parent's homes.

Now, independence is multifaceted and involves many different elements, including financial independence and health. Becoming financially independent goes beyond earning enough cash to live, though. It's about thinking about what we want to achieve with the money we earn and how we will continue to live a comfortable life when we can no longer earn money.

When we understand what consumerism robs us of, we can begin to define how much money we need to cover our financial needs not by working but by the interest we earn from the savings and investments we've created.

The Financial Superpowers in You!

With only eight states requiring financial literacy education, teens are banding together and calling for education in all things finance. In fact, 45% of American teens say that the way to a better financial future is through financial literacy training (Reinicke, 2020). Financial education reduces the widening financial opportunity gap for teens and young adults who feel that the subjects they're learning in school, while useful to specific careers, don't apply to the real world they need to face when they leave school.

As we know, change takes time, so what can we do about narrowing the financial opportunity gap right now? In the meantime, we can take the initiative and learn about personal finance by ourselves! Each of us has a hidden superpower within us to assimilate information and apply it to our lives. Reading this book and taking actionable steps to reclaim our financial future from the grips of the hybrid capitalist system we're living in is one of those steps. For us to take care of ourselves in the present and the future, it's important to understand how we can make our present money work for our future selves—with compounding interest.

Why Saving and Investing Matters

Instead of drilling information we've already discussed into your head, allow me to share a story about two young adults.

There are two sisters Nicole and Brandi. Nicole decided that she wanted to start saving for an early retirement at the age of 15. Brandi, 18 years old, landed a job that paid a very nice wage after graduating high school and started her YOLO philosophy (you only live once). Nicole, on the other hand, worked through high school, went to college, and started a decent career all the while executing her savings plan.

Twenty years later when Nicole turned 35, she had saved a total of $256,008! When Nicole told Brandi of her accumulation, Brandi was astonished. She immediately changed her approach to money as she had not saved a dime. She started to implement Nicole's savings plan and continued to do so in a disciplined fashion.

In the meantime, Nicole stopped contributing to her savings account and did not add another dime to her account. When Brandi turned 65, with an average of 6% interest over time, by sticking to Nicole's saving plan during that whole time, she had accumulated a total of $436,723.

When Nicole turned 65, the savings account that she had left alone 30 years prior had grown to a whopping $2,773,768! You may be wondering, how Nicole's account grew so much more than Brandi's. The answer is time for the power of compound interest to take its course. Brandi lost 20 years that if she had started when Nicole had as a teenager, she too would have been able to benefit more from compound interest.

To understand the true power of saving and compound interest over time, we need to first establish and become aware of the basic structure of effective saving.

The Fundamentals of Saving

To start off our discussion on how important it is to save, here is a quote from John Poole, "You must learn to save first and spend afterward."

The fundamentals of savings begin with first knowing what components are required to kick off your savings journey.

- **Income:** Having an income is the most important part of saving. Without income, saving can be frustrating and seem like an impossible thing to accomplish. This is why it is important to consider doing part-time jobs as a teenager to get ourselves started.
- **Creating a budget:** Creating a detailed budget that is practical to our needs is the best way to make saving manageable.
- **Set goals:** It is important to set goals for our savings because they reinforce our values and the importance of saving.
- **Creating an emergency fund:** Putting money away for emergencies allows us to leave our savings untouched so that it can continue to grow.

Once these fundamentals are in place, we can decide how much we're going to save. As mentioned before, deciding on an amount is difficult because our income may vary from week to week when we are working part-time. A better idea is to decide on a percentage.

Most people between the ages of 15 and 18 are in a unique position of not having many expenses for needs spending. Because of this, I'd suggest swapping the needs spending percentage of the 50-30-20 method and assigning this to savings.

That would mean our budgeting plan looks like this:

- 50% savings and investment
- 30% needs spending
- 20% wants spending

For teens who don't yet have the expense of an auto loan, I suggest setting aside 15% of needs spending as practice for monthly loan repayments. While this budget may sound very restricting, we still have money for ourselves under wants spending and we can practice delayed gratification when it comes to the larger purchases we want to make.

The average teen working part-time will earn about $365 per week. That's a total of about $1,500 per month. If 50% of this income was properly invested and saved using the power of compounding interest, the initial $750 investment would grow to just over $28,000. There are a lot of compound interest calculators online that can be used to work out how much money can potentially grow. This example was calculated with a $750 monthly contribution (50% of the $1,500 monthly wage) at an interest rate of 4% per year (Investor Tools, 2023).

For teens earning less than $1,500, compound interest on proper savings is still a formidable force. At $200 savings per month over 3 years, and 4% per annum, this investment grows to well over $7,000. By the 5-year mark, the $7,000 nearly doubles in value, and by the time 10 years pass, just shy of $30,000 is made.

Understanding Compound Interest

Let's begin by introducing simple interest. This is the interest paid on an amount deposited into most standard savings accounts. Simple interest is paid only on the capital (deposited amount) and accumulates at different intervals. For example, if $500 is deposited, the only interest earned would be on that $500 and not on any other interest earned.

Compound interest is when interest is earned on both the capital amount as well as any interest earned. So, if we were to deposit $500, instead of earning interest on only this amount, we would earn on the $500 plus the interest earned at the end of every annual cycle. For example, $500 would become $504 which would become $524, which would become $544, and so on. Some compound interest accounts offer varying frequency interest payments (monthly or quarterly) which grow an initial investment quicker.

The biggest pro to compound interest is that our money grows much quicker after the first year but the true magic of compound interest happens when we allow enough time for our money to grow exponentially. Remember the difference in the amount of money between Nicole and Brandi?

Compound interest works both on investments and debt and most of the time, debt that spirals out of control is because interest is compounded. A lot of private student loans work on compound interest which is why some people are still paying off their loans 30 years after graduating from college!

Investing Essentials

Investing is a bit more complex than saving but it offers more potential for building both short-term and long-term returns on small amounts of money used. Some investment options available to young adults under the age of 18 were introduced in Chapter 4, but it's important to know how to invest and what to invest in before placing our money into any investment option.

Perhaps the most important aspect of investing is knowledge. We must research the company or venue before investing. This could include business analysis, stock trends, and histories, understanding the volatility of an investment, and whether the risk outweighs the potential reward.

It's also very important to understand that no investment is a sure bet. While some investments do come with more security, nothing is guaranteed in the world of finance. This shouldn't deter us from investing—on the contrary. Instead, we need to look at investing as a balancing act where we diversify our savings and investments so that we create a financial safety net for ourselves.

For young adults, starting small in investment and focusing attention on compound interest savings options is a good way to begin experimenting with a diverse financial portfolio. High-risk investments that promise high rewards should be strongly discouraged because most young adults are prone to losing a lot of money in "get rich quick" schemes.

Instead of chasing the big payout, we need to focus on the long game, strategically placing our money in more sure return options and using the power of compound interest to our advantage. I would recommend accumulating $150,000 over time using this method before ever starting to invest in high-risk venues.

Investment Risk Management and Mitigation Strategies

Risk is a normal part of investing. Each of us has a certain tolerance to risk, and this tolerance is calculated based on several factors, including income, willingness to lose money, and investment knowledge. I've already mentioned that no investment is without some risk, but for young adults, a couple of mistakes can be avoided when deciding to invest.

- The first and biggest mistake young adults make when investing is deciding not to use their own money. Taking out a loan for investment purposes is just not a good idea. The reality is that repaying a loan sets us back and any low-risk investment takes time. The risk of not being able to offset loan repayments against long-term investment returns simply isn't worth it when it comes to young investors.
- The second mistake most young adults make is playing a market they're just not ready to invest in. I'm not denying that some investments pay and that a lot of people make money off playing the stock markets. The difference between young investors and people who capitalize on market volatility is experience and knowledge. Unless a teen has a sound knowledge of speculating and understands the market well, it's best to stay away from volatile investments.
- The final most common mistake is not understanding that all assets are not made equal. True assets are costly and the capitalist American Dream has always inferred that owning a property or properties is the pinnacle of a healthy financial standing. The reality is that property is a depreciating asset and unless we have the funds to upkeep the property while paying any monthly costs and installments, and I would argue generate an income from this property, investing in real estate can be a costly mistake for young investors. A better option for young investors wanting to enter into the real estate market is to look into real estate investment trusts (REITs).

Alternatively, we could consider duplex living so that we can rent while we own the property.

A Word on Investment Scams

We live in a world where a lot of the people we "know" we've never met. Gone are the days of walking into an investment firm to speak with a real-life broker, and even back then, people lost a lot of money to investment scam artists.

When it comes to investing, safe bets are always a better option and if it sounds too good to be true, it probably is. Never supply your personal information to someone you've just met on the internet and always consult with a trusted adult before investing. Look for companies that are well established and make sure you keep your identity safe, your passwords strong, and your wits about you!

Now that we have positioned ourselves to take full advantage of compound interest and our savings, how do we make that most important transition from high school to college? The next part of this book will prepare us for how we can do that.

Personal Finance Highlights

By internalizing these key lessons, teens can embark on their journey towards financial independence with confidence and resilience, equipped with the essential tools to navigate the complexities of the financial world.

1. Balancing Financial Realities and Curiosity: Instead of solely focusing on the struggles of the economy, we must strike a balance in our conversations with teens, emphasizing the importance of financial responsibility

while instilling curiosity about saving, investing, and compound interest.

2. Understanding Fear and Consumerism: Fear drives consumerism, leading to impulsive spending and neglect of financial security. By recognizing and overcoming fear-driven spending habits, we can prioritize disciplined saving and investing for a more secure future.

3. Empowering Financial Independence: Wealthy young adults understand the importance of preparing for the future without catastrophizing it. They embrace financial risks with confidence, leveraging investments and compound interest to secure their financial independence.

4. Harnessing the Power of Saving and Investing: Through a compelling story and practical examples, the significance of early saving and investing, particularly utilizing compound interest, is highlighted. Teens are encouraged to adopt disciplined saving habits to reap the long-term benefits of compound interest.

5. Investing Essentials and Risk Management: Young adults are urged to prioritize knowledge and caution in investing, avoiding common pitfalls such as using borrowed money, speculative investments, and overlooking asset quality. With prudent risk management strategies, they can navigate the investment landscape safely and build a robust financial future.

SHARE YOUR INSIGHTS, SHAPE THE FUTURE! UNLEASH THE STRENGTH OF KNOWLEDGE!

Dear Reader,

Your thoughts matter. By sharing your experiences and opinions, you're not only contributing to the ongoing conversation about financial literacy but also shaping the future for generations to come.

Your review of <u>The Personal Finance Choice for Teens and Young Adults</u> holds immense power. Robert F. Newkirk Jr.'s comprehensive guide empowers young minds to master money management and gain financial independence.

As the statistics show, the demand for financial education is on the rise among high school students, with a staggering 73% expressing a desire for more knowledge in this area (Turner, 2023). Yet, the reality is stark—many young adults are already burdened by debt before they even step foot into the workforce.

Imagine the impact we could make if every teenager had access to the tools and insights provided in this book. By writing a review, you're not just endorsing a product; you're advocating for change. You're championing the cause of financial literacy and taking a stand against the status quo.

As parents, guardians, and mentors, we hold the key to shaping a brighter future for the next generation. By demanding financial literacy education in schools and encouraging our children to take charge of their finances, we can equip them with the skills they need to thrive in an increasingly complex economic landscape.

Money is a powerful tool, but it's also slippery. With your help, we can empower young minds to navigate the pressures of capitalism and make informed decisions about their financial futures. Your review isn't just a rating; it's a call to action- to question the status quo and drive meaningful change.

Thank you for considering sharing your thoughts. Together, we can make a difference.

Warm regards,

Robert F. Newkirk Jr.

PART THREE
TRANSITIONING INTO ADULTHOOD (AGES 19-22)

When situations have you discombobulated,
"JUMP INTO THE POOL!"
That forces us to collaborate with other like-minded people.
*And when you get out of the pool, **MASTERMIND** it out!*

CHAPTER 6
SAVING FOR COLLEGE AND MANAGING STUDENT LOANS

From the age of 2, I have been fascinated by airplanes. My mother took me on a flight from Denver, CO, to Norfolk, VA, on a Boeing 727. I remember holding my mother's hand as we approached the stairs to get on the plane. That big old engine on top of the plane—I was hooked! I wanted to be a pilot when I grew up! But I had to go beyond just being a pilot. I wanted to know everything associated with aircraft—how the engines work, how are the wings designed, and what are the names of all the commercial and military aircraft.

In my senior year, I received a brochure for MIT, but I glossed over it. I'd never heard of the school before. My mother made me read it. The brochure talked about academics, varsity and intramural athletics, and so on. What caught my eye, though, was history was an elective credit. I elected not to take it!

I filled out the brochure to get a course catalog. In the catalog, I came across Course 16, aeronautical/astronautical engineering. At that time, my definition of an engineer was a train operator! So, this course had to be about transporting plane parts on trains! Sign me up! I applied and was accepted. *MIT*. Okay, great! Now, how are we going to pay for it?

Education forms part of our identity and a lack of access to it is a denial of expressing that identity. For many young adults over the age of 18, their choice of educational institutions directly affects their confidence, which changes the trajectory of their lives, and increases their perception of choice when it comes to future employment.

What we obtain in college becomes something that no one else can ever take from us. Education is confidence. Education is a new improved way of life. Education increases our power of choice. For many people, education is essential, but it comes at a high price that has to be effectively and efficiently navigated. And here's the cold truth: There are a lot of misconceptions when it comes to further education. We set self-limitation on what we can and cannot do to get a college education and sometimes, we set a trap for ourselves—one that has us paying for most of our adult lives.

Understanding College Costs

Between 1978 and 2015, college tuition costs rose 1,134%, the highest rising sector due to inflation, the second highest rising sector over the same period was Medicare at 607%. In 2023, the average cost of a college education was $36,436 per year in the US (Hanson, 2023). This cost does include some other education expenses, like books, supplies, and other daily expenses, but education costs vary wildly. Some of the most expensive colleges charge up to $80,000 per year!

Knowing how much a college education is going to cost and what extra costs might incur will help us plan properly for a financially secure future. With that in mind, let's take a look at some of these costs.

- **Tuition fees:** The cost of a particular course or the number of courses being taken each semester.
- **Books and supplies:** The cost of the textbooks a college uses in their program curriculum. This also includes other learning supplies like technology (laptops), software, and any practical equipment needed for the course (stationary, mathematical tools, scientific apparatus, and so on).
- **Boarding costs:** On or off-campus housing that needs to be paid for (rent)
- **Additional expenses:** All other expenses associated with college, like student medical plans, transportation, room furnishings, food, parking fees, Greek life, and so on.

Added to the above expenses, things like printing, tax, social groups, additional stationery and books, and food can catch us off guard. It's estimated that these extra costs set college students back about $500 every month and with the rising cost of living, this number is only set to increase.

Now I know this may sound like I am deterring you from college —I'm not—but you must understand that going to college is not as easy as taking out a loan and attending classes.

We need to be realistic about what education costs in a capitalist society, weigh the pros and cons of putting ourselves into debt, and understand that there are other ways to gain an education if we take the time to analyze our biases and set aside our preconceived misconceptions.

Saving for College: Starting Early

Having options when it comes to a college education is as empowering as the education itself. The rising costs of education shouldn't deter us from creating a solid plan for our future education.

There are many different ways we can attend college including applying for financial aid from colleges, other organizations, and the government alongside a proper college savings plan. We can still qualify for financial aid and student loans, *even* if we are saving, and the earlier the more control we have over our college options.

My recommendation is to obtain as many financial aid packages, scholarships, and grants as possible and allow the money that you saved to continue to grow with compound interest through college. Once college is completed and the loans are finally due, we can use future savings gains to pay off the loans leaving a substantial amount for starting a career.

Scholarships, Grants, and Financial Aid

Scholarships, grants, and financial aid for higher education do not only come from colleges and universities. There are financial sponsorship programs offered by individuals, private organizations, and federal and state governments.

Two scholarships I highly recommend researching are appointments to the military academies, military ROTC scholarships, and the private QuestBridge scholarship. The military academies are full four-year scholarships that are appointed with the recommendation from the senator of your state. ROTC scholarships are military-based and granted to the school you submit on your application if they have a detachment at that school. These are four-year scholarships that cover everything but room and board. Both the academy and ROTC come with a minimum four-year commitment to service in the military. QuestBridge is a full four-year scholarship worth over $200,000 each. The match scholarship recipients are granted admission to one of QuestBridge's college partners which includes several of the Ivy League schools and other top schools in the country.

These scholarships and grants are assumed to fill several different types of criteria. Starting early in high school is the best way to search around for scholarships and grants that we can qualify for. Getting financial aid usually involves filling out application forms and preparing for how to fill out these forms is the best way to improve the odds of landing a scholarship or grant. The most common types of forms are the Free Application for Federal Student Aid (FAFSA) and the CSS profile.

Financial aid is most commonly broken down into two categories:

1. **Merit-based financial aid:** Money that is awarded to those who have high academic or athletic achievement. This aid usually requires maintaining a minimum GPA or performing well on a school's sports team.
2. **Need-based aid:** Money that is set aside and allocated by the Federal government to households that fall below a certain income bracket. It's important to note that savings are not included in this bracket and even if we have money saved up for college and our future, we may still qualify for need-based financial aid.

We must check in with our adult guardians, discussing our education dreams. By chatting with the adults in our lives we can ascertain what employment benefits may cover higher education costs and grants and if scholarships are available to us. Added to this, having early discussions about our education needs allows us to take control of our financial future because we will know what options are available to us.

Understanding Financial Aid

Financial aid is designed to help potential students and their families defray higher education expenses. This aid is designed to cover tuition and fees as well as boarding costs, books and supplies, and other expenses.

Each of these types of aid is supplied through different sources, including high schools, federal and state agencies, colleges, foundations, and corporations. How much aid a person qualifies for depends on a specific set of guidelines that apply to the aid source. The type of aid received also determines how the student will need to repay the amount received. When aid is received, we can choose to accept or reject it based on our own set of criteria.

Federal student aid is applied for by filing an application (FAFSA) on the U.S. Department of Education's Federal Student Aid website. Forms must be filled out in October for the following academic year. Leaving your application until later in the year is risky, as additional documentation may need to be supplied. For students wanting to attend college in the fall, applications need to be submitted by June 30th in the same academic year.

Private colleges and some schools will require a supplemental form (CSS Profile) to be filled in. This form is used to determine how much of the college or school's own funds will be used for grants. These forms are notoriously more complicated and come with additional fees. Schools that require CSS Profiles can be found on the relevant College Board website. CSS Profile checks will do a much more comprehensive search into a family's finances and will take into account assets that are usually excluded on FAFSA checks.

A Word on Work-Study Aid

For students who are looking for another option when it comes to paying for their college tuition, work-study programs are available through some institutions. In a work-study program, students will apply for work usually on campus, to help a student cover their college-related expenses. Having said that, not everyone qualifies for work-study programs and each FAFSA applicant will need to demonstrate their financial need for the aid. The Federal minimum wage of $7.25 per hour is paid for work-study students and the average earnings for this study aid is $1,821 per month.

Responsible Borrowing: Student Loans 101

Access to student loans has increased to compensate for rising education costs. For responsible lenders, access to education loans can be a lifeline to attending a preferred college.

The education sector, however, has not been left untouched by rampant consumerism and capitalism, and we need to be mindful of why we want to attend a specific college—have we been enticed by marketing ploys and external pressures?

For many young adults, a college education will be their first large investment and purchase. Like any other investment, we must take a look at a couple of essential elements that will help us decide whether or not a loan is the right course of action. These include

- the interest rate applicable to the loan and how this will affect our repayment period.
- whether the interest applied to the original loan amount is fixed or variable.
- any penalties that may be applied to late payments.
- when a loan will need to be paid back—during studies or once a course is complete.

Being responsible with an education loan goes way beyond our spending though, and it's important to understand that everything from showing up to class daily, submitting assignments, and actively working toward achieving the academic results needed to excel in a chosen career.

In addition, we must examine our education needs by selecting the right school cost and career choice-wise, looking at and weighing up alternative schools (often cheaper colleges offer the same education), and choosing to live a minimalist lifestyle for the time we're at college. I recommend picking a college that ranks in the Newsweek Top 20 of the field of study you want to pursue. Other influences could be your parent's alma mater, a chance to play your favorite sport, or the geographical location of the school. My thought is if the school will not set you up for the career you want, what's the point in going into debt just because of tradition?

My suggestion is that regardless of the loan terms, payments should begin while at college to help reduce the capital amount owed. Spending frugally and choosing to pay before the loan is due will help shave *years* off of a loan's repayment period.

Do *not* cosign on someone else's loan! You do not want to be responsible for someone else's debt as well as your own. No matter how well you think you know someone, life happens, things change, and being lumped with someone else's student loan just isn't a smart move for your financial future.

Managing Student Loan Debt Effectively

Managing student debt effectively involves first knowing how much we can afford in terms of minimum repayments, due dates, and loan terms. Added to this, we need to have a solid plan in place to reduce the capital loan amount as often as possible to ensure we're not spending the better part of the next decade—yes, that's right 10 years of repaying for education!

Not being able to pay student debt can lead to some unpleasant consequences, including lowered credit scores, higher interest rates, and longer repayment terms. Paying off student loans 30 years after finishing college is not wildly impossible. The average amount of time people take to pay off their student loans is 21 years (Johnson, 2024). This is purely because they don't know better or haven't learned how to reduce and manage their student loan debt effectively.

Some of the most effective ways to manage student loans are listed below as well as what to do if we encounter financial difficulty. I would strongly encourage proper planning over debt crisis management, so make sure to save effectively and only make use of the safety nets provided under exceptional circumstances.

Tips to Reduce Student Loans

- **Pay more than the minimum.** An extra $50 payment into the capital amount of a student loan every month can reduce the loan period by two years. Always send extra payment separate from the original payment and label it as "Principal Only." Make use of online student loan calculators to visualize how effective additional payments are and budget for this additional amount.

- **Opt to pay bi-weekly instead of monthly.** Most people aren't aware that paying an installment every two weeks adds an extra payment to their loan amount each year. By making these bi-weekly payments, a loan's term can be reduced by an entire year, bringing a 10-year loan term down to 9 years.

- **Set up auto-pay.** Auto-pay loans sometimes offer a quarter-point interest rate discount. This might not sound like much of a discount but the hassle of remembering when to pay a loan, as well as the savings on interest, can considerably reduce loan repayment times. Making sure to set up bi-weekly payments and specifying that additional payments be added to the capital amount when using auto-pay can reduce a loan's payment time by half.

- **Use debt avalanche strategies.** For students with more than one loan, I don't recommend debt consolidation. Not only does this increase the minimum repayment amount making it more difficult to pay extra, but it also increases how long a loan needs to be paid back. Instead, make minimum repayments on debt with lower interest rates, opting to place extra cash into higher interest rate loans. Once high-interest loans are paid, repay the minimum amount plus the extra money on hand to the next loan, and so on until the largest debt is paid off.

- **Ask about assistance.** Once employed, ask about loan repayment assistance. Some employers may provide just over $5,000 to help pay off student debt. Make sure to place a percentage of any bonuses received straight into debt so that capital amounts can be reduced quickly.

What to Do When You Can't Pay

Sometimes, no matter how prepared we are, financial crises arise. When this happens, there are some options available as a safety net for student debt. They include

- debt payment deferments, where the loan period can be paused for a certain amount of time without accruing interest. Deferments are available when employed and living off government assistance.
- forbearance, which also pauses the loan repayment period for a certain amount of time but the interest continues to accrue. Forbearance should only be considered, therefore, when we do not qualify for deferment.
- income-driven repayment plans are a program that permits us to only meet absolute minimum payments. We must prove that we are living from paycheck to paycheck with no residual income. After 25 years of consistent payments, some may qualify for debt forgiveness.

Balancing Work and College

The idea of being a working student may sound like a drag but it opens the door to so many opportunities nonworking students aren't afforded. The key to balancing work and college lies in our ability to balance the academic and money-earning work we need to get done while still having a social life and having fun.

The biggest pro as a working student goes beyond simply being able to pay off education loans quicker and affording day-to-day expenses. Studies show that student employment leads to not only more money earned in college but also higher earning opportunities in the first year after college (Douglas, 2019).

These higher earnings are because working college students are gaining important real-world work skills that are valued by future employers. They already know how to show up on time, can effectively manage their time, and follow the directions required to do their assigned work. Essentially, working students already know what it takes to balance their lives through effective time management.

Time management is one of the most important muscles that you need to develop when you are in college. You are not in your parents' house anymore. They are not there to make decisions for you. For the first time, you are on your own. Choices in college are endless, from academic majors to recreational activities, intramural or varsity sports activities, social activities, and so on. If work becomes a part of the equation, time management is the only way that you can operate and not get behind in your studies or behind schedule in your work matters.

We must not enter into the workplace as a working student out of desperation but rather as part of an overall larger strategy that sets us up for a bright financial future. Working in college is *not*, however, an invitation to cast aside the consumerism-prevention strategies we've learned in previous years. Mature decision-making and choosing balance, as well as a minimalist life will ensure we are enjoying our time in college while still staying on track with our financial goals.

As seen from this chapter, financial planning is much easier to do when abundant resources are available. But how can we deal with it when resources are not enough? The next chapter will provide a detailed explanation of how to navigate such limiting financial situations.

Personal Finance Highlights

In essence, education is not just about what happens inside the classroom—it's about navigating the complexities of the financial landscape, making informed choices, and laying the groundwork for a prosperous future.

1. Empowerment through Education: Education is not merely a means to a career; it's an essential component of personal identity and empowerment. This chapter emphasizes that education shapes our confidence, life trajectory, and career choices, making it a fundamental aspect of personal development.

2. Facing the Reality of College Costs: The chapter presents a stark reality check on the soaring costs of higher education. Highlighting statistics on the exponential rise in tuition fees over the decades underscores the financial burden faced by aspiring students. By understanding the breakdown of college expenses, individuals can make informed decisions and plan effectively for their financial future.

3. Exploring Financial Aid Options: Amidst the daunting cost of college, there is a beacon of hope through various avenues of financial aid. From scholarships and grants to work-study programs and loans, there are diverse opportunities to alleviate the financial strain. By starting early and exploring all available options, individuals can access resources to pursue their educational aspirations.

4. Strategies for Responsible Borrowing: With access to student loans becoming more common, it is necessary to emphasize the importance of responsible borrowing. Understanding the implications of interest rates, repayment terms, and loan management strategies is

crucial in mitigating the long-term impact of student debt. By adopting prudent financial practices, individuals can navigate the complexities of student loans while minimizing their financial burden.

5. Balancing Work and Education: Being a working student isn't just about paying off loans—it's about gaining valuable real-world skills and setting the stage for future success. Effective time management, balanced decision-making, and a minimalistic lifestyle are essential for achieving academic and financial goals simultaneously.

CHAPTER 7
MANAGING LIMITED INCOME AND EXPENSES

Anthony Abraham Jack, a professor at the Harvard Graduate School of Education told a moving story of how he arrived at Amherst College in Massachusetts on a scholarship. Like so many other young adults, Jack wasn't adequately prepared to handle the financial pressures that came with student life even though he had received financial aid to cover his college tuition.

Back in the '90s, McDonald's ran $0.29 and $0.39 burger specials on Sundays—this became Jack's only form of sustenance during his family's trying times. However, there were no burger specials at college, and often, Anthony would go hungry. He was stranded with no way to travel back home to his family and went a lot of nights without food because the college did not offer meals during academic breaks.

To help cover the costs of staying on campus, Jack worked 10-hour shifts at the gym—at least the vending machines were fully stocked with junk snacks, a welcome change from the regular PB&Js he would get from the local CVS. Anthony admits that like so many students, he was blinded by the lights and trap of landing a spot at a coveted college.

As parents, it's important that we have open and honest discussions with our kids about what potential downfalls there are to college life outside of being able to pay back student loans. The consumer veil needs to be pulled back so that young adults can think more critically and analytically about what comes next.

Students without adequate financial literacy simply don't understand that there are so many costs that loans simply don't pay—regardless of what loan officers tell them as they sign the dotted line on paying back minimum installments for the next 10 years.

The cold, hard reality is that 65% of Americans are living from paycheck to paycheck with 35% of these people saying they run out of money before the next paycheck is even due (Batdorf, 2024). For a lot of students, Anthony Abraham Jack's story rings true, and if we ever hope to change this statistic, we need to start preparing young adults to navigate the world on a limited income before they're in college.

Navigating the World of Limited Income

Increases in tuition costs are well documented and as of the end of the second quarter in 2023, $1.77 trillion was owed in student loan debt (Schulz, 2023). Like Anthony, so many of us face the reality of becoming working students and living on a limited income while we study and transition into full independence.

Even with financial aid, the average student will require upwards of $500 in monthly costs for college expenses, and often, this amount doesn't cover traveling home to family or any leisure activities or expenses. When compared with the national average minimum wage, students need to work up to 17 hours per week to have enough money for living expenses outside of what their loan amounts cover—a tall ask when having to attend classes, submit assignments, and study for exams.

Efficient management of our limited funds ensures we can cover our needs and expenses while still saving for our future without hunting down PB&Js or going days without food, but it does mean developing self-discipline and readjusting old budgeting methods so that our paycheck sees us through.

Some may enter college aware of the fact that they will need to live frugally while others will buy into the consumer television dream of endless parties and a lifestyle free of responsibilities. A realistic, balanced viewpoint where we prepare before college and begin living within our means is absolutely essential if we're to enjoy this phase of our lives.

My suggestion would be to temporarily shelve the 50-30-20 budget used in our earlier teens and readjust to a more sensible budget of 40-30-30. Before breaking this down, it's important to understand each person's needs are different. Some may enter into college with more financial leeway while others will have to commit to being extremely restricted. Because of this, assessing our expenses monthly to analyze where our money goes will need to become a college habit.

A 40-30-30 budget is broken down as follows:

- 40% of *surplus* income should be saved.
- 30% of *surplus* income should be put away for emergencies.
- 30% of *surplus* income should be set aside for wants/fun spending.

It's entirely up to us as individuals how we will split our surplus income, but we should be aware of our financial goals and regularly assess where our money is going so that we can remain in a good financial position.

The consumer-capitalism hybrid system we live in may be designed to entice us to buy but that doesn't mean there aren't advantages to this system that we can exploit to our advantage as students on a limited income. Some of the ways we can save money while in college include

- buying second-hand textbooks, checking for downloadable copies, or copies of books that have exclusive digital access at a reduced price.
- making use of campus libraries.
- using student discounts for everything from food to stationery and necessary clothing items.
- planning meals ahead of time and shopping around for budget meal items.
- choosing to cut back on monthly subscription packages including phone bills.
- using public transport where possible.

Slashing bills and expenses may require some thought and careful planning but for most students, it can be done. For those of us who don't have the privilege of being able to cut back on any additional expenses, self-discipline will become our greatest ally in college— and it all comes down to properly tracking our expenses.

Tracking Expenses

I was a brand-new 2nd lieutenant in the Air Force and my first travel assignment was to Princeton, NJ. I was shadowing this 1st Lieutenant to a Program Management Review which went for the day. That night, he thought he was doing me a favor by taking me to New York City to hit the bars and go clubbing for the night. What amazed me was how reckless he was with his money, drinking and making it rain for no reason. He even told me to live it up because we were on "per diem." Somehow, I succumbed a little to the peer pressure. When I got back from the trip, I realized that my total travel budget for that trip was clearly in the red. It was at that moment that I vowed to never again lose money on a business trip. I committed that on every trip, I would make money off of that per diem. I never did lose money on a business trip again.

College will present us with moments that could influence, deter, or sway our focus. No one is saying that we should be perfect. It is human nature to make mistakes but we need to make a conscious effort to learn from these bumps in the road and choose to rectify our behavior as quickly as possible.

Tracking our expenses by regularly reviewing and analyzing our bank account provides us with the unique opportunity to find where we may be losing money and where we are being enticed into expenses that just aren't necessary. Regular analysis also ensures we stay ahead of the curve so that we can adjust our expenses where necessary, especially when it comes to variable expenses.

Making adjustments may be difficult, especially for students who are already on an extremely tight budget, but splitting budgets into the three necessary categories for financial health and self-discipline can help us uncover our financial mistakes so that we can actively rectify any consumer behaviors we may have slipped back into.

Setting Financial Goals on Limited Income

Our expenses aren't the only aspects that will need to be adjusted while we're in college. We'll also need to tweak our financial goals. Now, I'm not saying we need to abandon our mid- and long-term goals, but we do need to be realistic about what we can achieve with a limited income.

I would suggest leaving mid- and long-term goals untouched as these should already include the plans laid to pay off student loans in a shorter frame of time and any future investments. Instead, we need to tweak our short-term goals opting to live frugally and spend our money wisely.

We need to understand that we are not denying ourselves a college experience. We can still have fun and get the best out of our experience while in college. What we do need to do is let go of our expectations and the preconceived ideas that have been planted in our heads with the express purpose of pushing us into a debt trap in this early phase of our lives. Ultimately, it's the small steps (savings) that count and accumulate into wealth and financial freedom. As Confucius (n.d.) said, "It doesn't matter how slowly you go so long as you don't stop."

Frugal Living and Smart Spending

Frugality is often confused with being miserly or stingy but a quick look at the definition of the word lets us know that its true meaning is to be economical. In financial literacy, there are a lot of words that have been *deliberately* formulated to instill negative beliefs to derail our financial success.

Being frugal doesn't mean you automatically default to the cheapest on the market—remember, quality is always preferable over quantity. Smart spending and frugal living work hand in hand—shopping around, making use of discounts, choosing to purchase items that are good quality and will last, delayed gratification, and so on.

Frugality is a mental mindset—a blueprint to financial success, it's not being "cheap" or stingy. Buying the generic brand "Kola" over Pepsi Cola because it is on sale for a dollar less is cheap. Being frugal is simply being wise when we spend money. I consider myself frugal, but if I am committed to buying something, it is usually the best brand on the market that meets my requirements of need. Every dollar that I spend, I consider an investment. Splurging is unheard of unless I have determined way ahead of time that it is an absolute need.

Investing for Limited Income Earners

In the early stages of investing, it is important to focus on investments that have less risk and make it easier to accumulate capital without having to constantly monitor the stock market in case a bear market shows up. I recommend a limited income earner to put as much money as possible into an index fund and build it up to $10,000 over time before thinking about more aggressive investments in the stock market.

Investing in stocks can appear to be a promising idea, but as I explained in Chapter 5, market volatility can lead to financial loss, especially if we lack the capacity to keep up with market analysis. Assuming that a total of at least $150,000 has been saved and investment is something of interest, opting for low-risk, long-term investments would be the most suitable choice.

For now, our focus needs to be placed on living within our means and enjoying a college experience on limited resources. But how do we navigate around the pressure colleagues might present who have more resources than we do and we want to hang out with them? The next chapter addresses this issue with a basic breakdown of how to keep an active social life in college while maintaining financial discipline.

Personal Finance Highlights

Navigating the world of limited income during college requires a combination of financial literacy, disciplined budgeting, smart spending habits, and forward-thinking investment strategies. By embracing these principles and staying vigilant in managing their finances, students can not only survive but thrive in the face of financial challenges, paving the way for a brighter and more secure future.

1. Facing the Reality of College Life: Anthony Abraham Jack's poignant story serves as a powerful reminder that the glitz and glamour of college can often mask the harsh reality faced by many students. From struggling to afford meals to working long hours just to cover basic expenses, Jack's experience underscores the importance of acknowledging and preparing for the financial challenges of higher education.

2. The Importance of Financial Literacy: As parents and educators, we must engage in open and honest discussions with young adults about the financial realities of college life. Beyond student loans, there are numerous hidden costs that students may not be aware of, highlighting the critical need for financial literacy education to empower students to make informed decisions.

3. Efficient Management of Limited Funds: With the staggering rise in tuition costs and student loan debt, efficient management of limited funds becomes essential for survival. The 40-30-30 budgeting approach offers a practical framework for students to prioritize saving,

emergency funds, and discretionary spending, ensuring financial stability and resilience amidst financial constraints.

4. Strategies for Smart Spending: Embracing frugality does not equate to deprivation but rather entails making wise and intentional spending choices. From purchasing second-hand textbooks to taking advantage of student discounts, adopting smart spending habits can significantly alleviate financial strain without compromising on quality of life.

5. Investing for the Future: While immediate financial pressures may seem overwhelming, it's crucial to lay the foundation for future financial security. Starting with low-risk investments like index funds allows students to gradually build wealth over time, setting the stage for long-term financial success beyond the college years.

CHAPTER 8
SMART SPENDING HABITS WHILE NAVIGATING PEER PRESSURE

A s our kids begin navigating college, we expect them to deal well with peer pressure, but we fail to understand that college pressures are different from those they experience in high school. College brings with it a new set of temptations, ones that are not fraught with the consequences of being underage or being grounded.

At this age, kids truly are young adults and that means testing the limits of what is acceptable (or not) in terms of living an independent adult life. While a lot of emphasis is placed on the consequences of life-endangering decisions, not enough time is spent discussing the financial pressure young adults will face while navigating this phase of their lives.

Students who come from a better financial standing, social media, and preconceived ideas of what college *should* be can all influence how our young adults shape their college experience. Our young adults are not immune to the consumerism tactics that bamboozle us into "regret purchases" and additional costs. Something as simple as a game console that was purchased *responsibly* from wants savings can quickly spiral into uncontrolled additional monthly subscription and upkeep costs.

We, at the very least, have experience behind us, and hindsight, as we know, is 20/20. College exposes young adults not only to having to navigate the world independently but to a different form of peer pressure as they encounter and interact with people from diverse cultural, religious, and financial backgrounds. Values and beliefs clash at a time when many are still battling with the formation of their adult identity and oftentimes, the subtle art of saying no succumbs to the burning desire to fit in and belong.

The Art of Saying "No"

It is not easy to say the word "no" and go about our business. Financial peer pressure presents itself in different forms. We need to develop the habits and attitudes that facilitate the art of saying "no" so that we can commit to our financial goals. And make no mistake, even if we say no, pressure is likely to increase. Some peers may resort to taunting us into participating while others try to draw out an explanation. Let me make it clear, we *never* need to explain our financial situation or goals to anyone. When in doubt, I like to use the declaration, "I will not blame, complain, or justify my situation," as a reminder to be assertive when dealing with peer pressure.

Building assertiveness begins by recognizing and honoring our values and making a decision upfront about what financial habits we will engage in. Keep in mind, the decisions that we make when we are 20 years old, we will have to live with when we are 40! By aligning our financial habits with our values, we can more clearly see who is having a positive financial influence on us and who isn't. The reason for this is that explanations surrounding financial peer pressure are often general. These explanations offer no direct value, nor do they highlight the impact financial pressure can have on us—no wonder I was confused when the 1st Lieutenant wanted to "make it rain," for no reason. It was my reflection after this incident that encouraged my assertiveness.

I'm not denying that assertiveness in setting our financial boundaries can lead to severed friendships. In college, some friends may have more money and will "splash their cash" more readily, but often, these people develop in maturity at some point and may feel that they are being taken advantage of or may expect the same in return.

Assertive conversations about financial goals and spending expectations will help to iron out any spending disparities and ultimately, may solidify a friendship, evolving it into a mature adult exchange where two parties respect each other's decisions.

Assertiveness ensures that rather than trying to fit in with everyone, we can align our college friendships with people who both respect us and whose values align with our own. This doesn't mean we can't enjoy our college experience—on the contrary! Mature, respectful relationships allow us to become creative with our time and our money, and who knows, perhaps you even become the go-to guy or gal for college financial advice.

Avoiding Spending Temptation

No one is immune to college spending temptation. Having said that, there are ways to avoid spending temptation while still enjoying ourselves. A great way to avoid temptations and evaluate whether something warrants parting with our money is to compare experiences. Here are a few examples:

- Going out drinking may sound like a fun college experience, but often, there's nothing to show for it—not even the memory of the night. Rather than wasting huge amounts of money on something that has no value, we could consider low-cost activities, like road trips, picnics, or game nights, where we can make lasting memories and solidify our friendships.

- Credit cards seem to be a status item when in college, but having a card on hand, even if it's a regular debit card, can lead to overspending when tempted. Instead, we can opt to work out how much we intend to spend, take cash with us, and leave our cards at home. When the cash is gone, it's gone, and we're more likely to be mindful of how we're spending.
- Be aware of discounts. Student discounts can be incredibly handy when working within a budget but they can also be the source of huge temptation. Instead of purchasing something that is 50% off that you wouldn't ever pay full price for, opt for logical discounts on items that are *needed*. Fifty percent off of something you don't need is still money wasted!

Navigating Consumerism and Advertising in College

When I first started my time in the military, I was always perturbed when coworkers asked me if I wanted to go to So-and-So's "going away luncheon" whom I didn't even know. I was stationed in sunny California in the high-rent district on a beginning Lieutenant's salary. I was not trying to spend $10+ every time somebody had a going away luncheon. But peer pressure was immense. I had to find a way out. My solution was that I would go to the gym at lunchtime so that I had an official excuse to say no. I ended up meeting a whole new cadre of people who thought the same as me in that regard. The only going away luncheon I would attend from then on was for people that I worked out in the gym with who had gotten their permanent change of station papers!

Consumerism preys on unsuspecting college students in a whole lot of different ways. From luncheons, like my story above, to gadgets, food, and clothes that wouldn't normally appeal to us, consumerism and advertising are designed to entice young adults. The reason for these tactics is debatable—perhaps taking advantage of us in a vulnerable financial and psychological time of our lives, or simply to ensnare us in a debt trap from early on in our lives.

I'd like to say that as we get older, we become less susceptible to advertising, but this simply isn't true because we need to know how consumerism's tactics are delivered (the medium) and what adverts do *to* us just to entice a purchase.

Modern adverts targeted at college students are delivered by

- print advertising
- streaming, television, radio, and podcasts
- direct mail in the form of paper or catalogs, brochures, and emails
- pop-up advertising while browsing
- pay-per-click advertising and sponsored ads on search engines
- social media and influencer advertising
- product placement and color enticement in physical and online stores
- outdoor ads including billboards, the sides of busses, and so on

Once we know how these adverts are delivered to us, we can begin to uncover what they're designed to do. For in-store advertising, color and product placement are incredibly powerful but subtle subconscious purchasing influencers For example, while I was creating my online money management course, I worked at a grocery store stocking shelves and setting up marketing billboards and displays. If we had an overstock of bananas, we would set up tables just for bananas right as you entered the produce section. Management would determine the sale price of the bananas and we would place yellow signs as you enter the store. Also, there were specialty cases throughout the store placed strategically to make sure all customers were subconsciously aware bananas were on sale even if they only came to purchase paper towels. Don't believe me? Take the time to consciously become aware of your surroundings the next time you're in a store and look out for subliminal advertising cues.

The key to unlocking a life where you're less influenced by consumerism-driven marketing and advertising begins with becoming mindful and aware. Once you're no longer being subliminally influenced, you can begin to unravel the manipulation being used. These manipulation and advertising tactics are not new.

The difference, however, between what our parents and grandparents experienced is the *frequency and pervasive force of consumerism.* In the past, ads reached audiences through a limited number of mediums that could mostly be ignored unless we were looking to purchase. Now, advertising is *everywhere* and permeates every corner of our lives, even when our electronic devices are switched off.

Sustaining Smart Spending Habits

Educating ourselves about consumerism and subliminal advertising tactics is the first step to freeing ourselves from the clutches of regretful purchasing and debt. Having said that, there are other ways we can continue to dull our response to the onslaught we will face for the remainder of our adult lives. Here's how:

- Dedicate and commit to the continuous learning process of financial literacy—there will *always* be something new designed to entice you, so stay one step ahead.
- Consider your financial, personal, and professional goals and value these above any purchase that may prevent you from achieving them.
- Expand your perspective and understand that perspectives can and *do* change. If you live a life based on a fixed mindset, you'll fall into consumer traps more regularly than those with a growth mindset.
- Think with your head and not your heart—emotions are primal and powerful. Evoking emotions is intended to override conscious, rational thought processes. Instigate the 24-hour rule *every* time you have an emotional response to an advert or influencer.
- Appreciate the value of data—if your budget shows you're spending wildly or you could save, chances are that you're being influenced on a subliminal level. Trust the numbers!
- Use your budget for future decisions and not just present ones—what you spend today will affect you tomorrow.

Being able to master psychology and the art of saying no while sticking to low-cost social activities is a great way to maintain a healthy financial situation. The bottom line is we still have to address the hefty objectives of dealing with college costs. How do we address the big-ticket items? The next chapter will provide us with some answers!

Personal Finance Highlights

By mastering the art of saying no, building assertiveness, avoiding spending temptations, navigating consumerism, and sustaining smart spending habits, you'll be equipped to thrive in college while staying true to your financial objectives.

1. The Art of Saying No: Developing the ability to say "no" assertively is crucial in maintaining control over your finances. Remember, you don't owe anyone an explanation for your financial decisions. By aligning your spending habits with your values, you can confidently navigate peer pressure without compromising your goals.

2. Building Mature Relationships: Assertiveness in financial matters can lead to deeper, more respectful friendships. By engaging in open, honest conversations about financial goals and expectations, we can strengthen relationships with like-minded individuals who respect our financial decisions.

3. Avoiding Spending Temptations: While college presents countless spending temptations, there are strategies to resist them without sacrificing enjoyment. From opting for low-cost activities to being mindful of discounts, you can make intentional choices that align with your financial priorities.

4. Navigating Consumerism and Advertising: Educate yourself about the tactics of consumerism and advertising to become more mindful and resistant to their influence. By understanding how ads target you and being aware of subliminal cues, you can make informed decisions and resist impulse purchases.

5. Sustaining Smart Spending Habits: Commit to continuously learning about financial literacy and staying ahead of consumer trends. Keep your financial, personal, and professional goals at the forefront of your decision-making process and rely on data and budgeting to guide your spending choices.

CHAPTER 9
TACKLING STUDENT LOANS AND COLLEGE COSTS

Most parents who have raised kids successfully to college age fall into two categories—those who remember the endless struggle of paying back student loans (perhaps still paying these loans) and those who seem to have forgotten. To complicate matters, parents born in the '70s and '80s weren't subject to the exorbitant cost of tertiary education. Back then, college cost, on average, $11,840 per year for a 4-year degree. Today, it runs over $30,000 per year (Rivera, 2023).

For young adults who haven't acquired the financial knowledge and literacy they *require* to navigate exorbitant costs of living, student loans can become a never-ending debt trap—one they can feel they will never be free of. As parents, we need to be sympathetic to the new challenges young adults face and be prepared to give the right advice and *solutions* that pertain to these financial hurdles.

We *cannot* become stuck in the way we did things because life is different. While some solutions, like compound interest, are universal and still work, the cold hard reality is that paying off debt today is far more difficult than it was 20 or 30 years ago. I'm not denying the interest rate hikes of the '80s (eight percent!) made things tough; the temptation to spend was less and the disparity between what we earned and what we needed to pay back was less.

The Higher Education Dilemma

A survey conducted shows that two-thirds of Americans believe that higher education simply isn't worth the cost to students anymore (Tough, 2023). I would argue that it is not the state of American education that is the problem but the nature of the capitalist-consumerism hybrid economy that has negatively impacted our viewpoints on higher education. The rising cost of living, the stark reality of how long it will take to pay off our education, and the disparity between wage increases and the cost of living have skewed our perceptions.

A college education, without a doubt, has benefits for us, but we need to understand the systemic nature of the economic times we live in so that we can properly manage our student debt and college costs. Instead of looking at the bigger picture, which can be quite overwhelming, we need to break things down into smaller, more manageable actions we can take at the moment. This allows us to secure a healthy financial future while still enjoying the *privilege* of a higher education.

Before continuing with this chapter, I would like to make one thing abundantly clear: College is not for everyone. If you're not interested in college, would prefer a trade school education, or would like to obtain your higher education qualification through other means, that's great! The world would be a very different, chaotic space if we were to all hold a degree and no one had an interest in service or trade-related work.

When I was running my Aerospace Flight Academy, I had a student who was bored out of his mind during the first part of the Aviation Career Education Camp week. As the week progressed, all of the other students in the camp had been encapsulated by the activities we had to offer, but not him. He was bored to the point where it hurt my feelings. But on Friday, we visited the Aviation Maintenance Institute. Aircraft engines, propellers, maintenance— his eyes lit up that day. He was hooked! Got 'em! He was destined for trade school and maintaining aircraft engines. He just needed to be exposed.

I would encourage every one of us to free ourselves of the capitalist notion that those who choose a trade career are somehow *below* us or are miserable with their chosen career path because they did not obtain a degree.

Understanding Types of Student Loans

Chapter 8 introduced us to the two types of loans available to us. Within each of these two loan categories are subtypes that dictate the interest payable, when interest begins to accrue, when first payments are due, and amounts that can be borrowed. For those of us who want to attend college and will require a student loan, we must understand the type of loan being taken and how it will affect us directly and in the future.

Types of Federal Student Loans

There are four main types of federal student loans available to college students.

1. **Direct subsidized loan:** Available to undergraduate students who can demonstrate financial need. Interest is

not charged while the student is at school and with a six-month grace period after graduation.

2. **Direct unsubsidized loan:** Available to undergraduate and graduate students with *no* financial needs requirements. Interest begins to accrue from day one of accessing the loan and may or may not have a payment deferment period.

3. **Direct PLUS loan:** Available to students and parents of students, graduate and undergraduate, who have maxed out direct unsubsidized loan limits. Loans cover the full cost of attendance but *not* other financial aid.

4. **Direct consolidation loan:** Available to students who wish to consolidate several different student loans, combining each of these to form one capital and interest amount.

Interest rates for federal student loans are fixed each year by the U.S. Congress. These interest rates are based on the 10-year Treasury note yield and while they may vary from year to year, once a loan is approved, interest may not fluctuate. Currently (2023/2024), loan rates are

- **Direct subsidized loan:** 5.50%
- **Direct unsubsidized loan:** 5.50% for undergraduates and 7.05% for graduates
- **Direct PLUS loan:** 8.05%
- **Consolidation loan:** Percentage rates vary based on the lending institution and can be as low as 5.8% peaking at over 15%.

The capital sum we are permitted to borrow will vary based on several factors. These factors are listed in the table below.

	Dependent undergraduate student	Independent undergraduate student	Graduate or professional degree student
Year 1	$5,500 with up to $3,500 that can be subsidized.	$9,500 with up to $3,500 that can be subsidized.	Full education cost if needs be.
Year 2	$6,500 with up to $4,500 that can be subsidized.	$10,500 with up to $4,500 that can be subsidized.	Full education cost if needs be.
Year 3 and beyond	$7,500 with up to $5,500 that can be subsidized.	$12,500 with up to $5,500 that can be subsidized.	Full education cost if needs be.
Lifetime maximum limit	$31,000 with up to $23,000 that can be subsidized.	$57,500 with up to $23,000 that can be subsidized.	Full education cost if need be.

Private Student Loans

Private student loans are offered by several lending institutions and while the lending terms are similar to federal loans, some differences can affect our financial health. The largest financial health factor we need to consider when it comes to private loans is interest.

Interest rates charged on private student loans are based on credit scores, and interest begins accumulating as soon as a loan is granted. For students who do not have an adequate credit history or other lending criteria history, a cosigner may be required.

Private student loans generally cover the total cost of college attendance including tuition, fees, room and board, supplies, books, and so on. Federal loans, however, are limited to under-graduates as per the amounts above.

Loaned amounts will be sent to the student's preferred college and a loan cannot exceed the costs associated with college attendance. In other words, our student loan is not an invitation to spend wildly on items that have nothing to do with our tertiary education.

Scholarships and Grants

The words scholarship and grant are often used interchangeably but some key differences set them apart. While both are considered to be gift aid money, scholarships are awarded on merit while grants are awarded on financial need.

Scholarships

A scholarship is granted based on merit for exceptional performance in academics, arts, athletic talent, and so on. Most of the time, scholarships are awarded by private providers and organizations that set aside money to educate future talent. Having said that, some colleges award full tuition based on academics (GPA), admissions test scores, and class rank if applicable. Scholarships are available to undergraduate and graduate students (fellowships). Scholarships are taxable and are used to pay tuition fees, textbooks, and living expenses.

In 2021, just under $100 million in scholarship money was left unclaimed purely due to a lack of application (Johnson, 2023). Again, one could argue that the stigma attached to scholarships and grants is the driving force behind students not seeking gift aid. Or perhaps, it is a lack of financial literacy education that is the driving force behind unclaimed educational money. The fact of the matter is that both grants and scholarships can be used to supplement our college savings and reduce the cost of our debt. When it comes to college tuition fees, every dollar earned in grants and scholarships is a dollar saved in cash we don't have to borrow.

Grants

Financial grants are awarded to students who demonstrate financial need according to different criteria. These criteria include the difference between the expected cost of attendance. The Federal Pell Grant is based primarily on SAI. It's important to note that grants are awarded by the federal and state governments as well as by colleges.

Maximizing Financial Aid and Scholarships

Financial aid statistics show that more than 80% of college students apply for some form of financial aid program (Hanson, 2020). With the rising cost of college education, the vast majority of students and their parents rely on a combination of student loans, savings, and financial aid to help them cover tuition costs. For many students, receiving a financial aid award letter warrants celebration and relief as some financial burden is lifted.

To maximize financial aid and scholarships, we must first commit to applying early and ensuring we meet the criteria of the scholarship or grant programs applied for. Although the vast majority of students will wait until the October opening date for FAFSA submissions, we can apply as early as February the year before college admissions to qualify. Once accepted, it's important to assess the criteria on which we were awarded the aid. The reason for this is financial aid is determined by income earned two years prior. Financial circumstances change and we may qualify for more aid based on new financial hardships or situations.

Added to grants, we can begin sourcing merit-based scholarships. Stats show that on average, every 40 hours spent searching and applying for scholarships will result in $10,000 secured college income (Hanson, 2020). These 40 hours can most productively be used by

- searching and applying for local scholarships.
- applying for smaller scholarship awards.
- taking the time to put together a body of work that includes essays, projects, and videos. Scholarships that require more work have fewer applicants and are more likely to be awarded to students who take the time and effort needed to apply.
- ensuring honesty in applications.
- being original and showcasing personality.
- ensuring all requirements are satisfied correctly and accurately—proofread your work!
- submitting applications early.
- never giving up—apply for as many scholarships as possible.

Navigating the College Selection Process

College application fees can become excessive and wasteful. Remember that you can only attend one college. My recommendation is to narrow the search down to five colleges to apply to, with one of the five serving as your fail-safe college, which you are positive will accept you. Choose these colleges based on the following criteria:

- The school is in the top 20 schools in the field you're interested in studying.
- The school is in the region of the country with the climate you prefer—you'll be living there for the majority of your time for the next four years.
- Favorable sports program (varsity and intramural) if you are athletically inclined and your ability compares with NCAA Divisions I, II, or III.

- Size of the student population that you would prefer to be a part of—a college of 1,000 students versus 50,000 students.

Once you have a list of schools, you can begin to evaluate the cost of your education to narrow down your selection to five preferred colleges. This can be done by comparing the *cost to the value and experience* received at selected colleges.

At this point, it's also important to begin applying for scholarships and grants to offset the cost of tuition. Not many prospective college students know that gift aid is available before they have been accepted into a school, especially for scholarship purposes. The sooner you apply for scholarships and grants, the easier it becomes to plan your finances accordingly.

While four years may seem like an eternity now, your days in college will pass by swiftly. Busy schedules tick time away and by properly selecting and preparing for your college experience, you can truly seize every moment.

Alternatives to College

As I mentioned before, college is not for everyone, and with the rising financial cost of education, some may need to seek alternatives to a traditional college experience. Between 2020 and 2023, 55% of graduating high school students chose not to go to college with a quarter of these students opting for associate degrees (Claybourne, 2024). The remainder of the high school students interviewed selected the alternative tertiary education paths listed below.

- **Vocational and trade schools:** Education institutions that provide in-depth knowledge based on skills. Examples of these schools include culinary school, auto, dental, law enforcement, and so on.

- **Self-paced schooling:** A lot of careers don't require formal education but do value some form of recognized qualification. Self-paced education for careers in coding, animation, production, design, and so on are still very lucrative careers without requiring a degree.
- **Apprenticeships and internships:** Jobs that are more hands-on, like electrical and plumbing work, personal assistant work, and even rig jobs, don't require a degree and employees prefer practical learning. Entry-level pay for apprenticeship and internship jobs may be low but with time and experience, these jobs pay as much and sometimes more than some degree jobs.
- **Military:** To qualify for the military, students must take the Armed Services Vocational Aptitude Battery (ASVAB), a test that measures their aptitude for certain skills. Once accepted into the military, students have access to a wide variety of tertiary education programs that can be applied to college credits. However, my recommendation is that if you are seriously considering the military, go to college on a ROTC scholarship to become a commissioned officer if you want the opportunity to make the top rank in the military. If you enlisted out of high school, you would become a noncommissioned officer, which is good for a respectable career, but you will never have the chance to make the top rank.
- **Online colleges:** For some degrees, in-person instruction is not necessary, nor is a full-time commitment. There are several online college degree programs available at a reduced cost. This allows students to juggle their personal commitments, maintain a job, and study without the added cost of living on campus.

- **Job-specific degrees:** Many students choose to find a junior position in a company that will invest in training, education, and advancement opportunities. Many companies in the US focus on growing emerging talent rather than focusing on a degree. This allows students to increase their earnings as they become educated at a reduced cost.

Getting through college can happen fast. Now, how do we handle the rest of the future after college? Part IV of this book will provide a thorough breakdown.

Personal Finance Highlights

In essence, while college remains a valuable option for many, understanding the full spectrum of educational opportunities and financial strategies empowers individuals to make informed decisions that align with their aspirations and financial well-being. By acknowledging the evolving landscape of education and finance, we can better equip ourselves and future generations for success in an ever-changing world.

1. Understanding the Changing Landscape: The cost of tertiary education has dramatically risen over the past few decades, leaving many young adults burdened with student debt. Parents must acknowledge these new challenges and equip themselves with the right knowledge to guide their children through these financial hurdles.
2. Recognizing the Value of Higher Education: While the rising costs may lead some to question the value of higher education, it's essential to understand that the problem lies not in education itself, but in the economic system surrounding it. By comprehending the systemic nature of

our economic times, we can better manage student debt and college costs.

3. Systemic Economic Realities: Understanding the systemic nature of today's economic climate is paramount. Rising living costs, stagnant wages, and the disparity between education expenses and income levels reshape our perceptions of higher education's value and affordability.

4. Maximizing Financial Aid: By leveraging federal student loans, private loans, scholarships, and grants, students can mitigate the financial burden of college tuition. Applying early and diligently seeking out merit-based scholarships can significantly reduce the need for excessive borrowing.

5. Exploring Alternatives: College is not the only path to success. Vocational and trade schools, self-paced education, apprenticeships, military service, online colleges, and job-specific degrees offer viable alternatives worth considering. Embracing diverse educational pathways ensures individuals find the best fit for their interests, skills, and career goals.

PART FOUR
ENVISIONING THE FUTURE
(AGES 23-28)

When all else fails,
"JUMP INTO THE POOL!"
That forces us to fail on our way to success.
*And when you get out of the pool, **WORK** it out!*

CHAPTER 10
COLLEGE GRADUATION TO CAREER PLANNING

Preparing for life after college is both daunting and exciting. Finding work within the field we've studied, the prospect of solidifying long-term relationships, and, as parents, letting go of the idea that our kids will come back to the nest all become a reality. Our fledglings *should* be ready to take on the world, navigating the unique challenges adults face. We tell ourselves that if we have done our jobs as parents correctly, success is on the horizon for young adults.

We hope they have been instilled with enough resilience and forethought to make good decisions for themselves and stick by them, and we sometimes cloud over the fact that modern young adults are entering into a job market that has evolved quite substantially since we went door-to-door, resume in hand.

Recent statistics show that young adults face an uphill battle when trying to find a job, with a success rate of 8.54% (Brackett, 2021). To put that into perspective, young adults need to apply for between 100 and 200 jobs at a rate of 6 applications per day, every day of the week to secure work.

The cold, hard reality is that as young adults graduate college, they face not only paying back their college education loans but also the pressure of finding work before their first installment is due. For those prepared or lucky enough to have a decent amount of savings, the prospect of securing their independence is just as daunting.

We need to be empathetic toward this new struggle and be prepared to instill in our young adults the formula for employment success—Prepare + Persevere + Patience = Success.

Life After College: Repayment and Beyond

Graduation day is upon us and a new metamorphosis awaits. For those who have college loans with a deferment period, the joy of graduating is tempered by the pressure to find employment. We're entering into a transition period and a stark realization that we've done it—we're independent adults and our lives are entirely our responsibility.

College is a safe space, a no-man's land somewhere between childhood and adulthood. For the most part, we're free to be creative and make mistakes in college without the repercussions and financial realities we now face. It's not, however, all doom and gloom! There is a way to use this transitional period to our advantage so that we can set ourselves up for success.

- **Understand that success takes time.** Most of us have been indoctrinated by social media to believe that success comes overnight. It doesn't, nor is there a set definition for success. Success is whatever we individually define it to be and future goals and success will take time to achieve in the same way it took time and effort to graduate from college.

- **Start living life with intent.** Up until now, intentional living has probably been reserved for financial, career, and life-changing decisions. For us to become successful, we need to expand this intentional living to other aspects of our lives. From maintaining relationships to big-ticket purchases, like a home, living with intent will ensure we're always making the right decision for ourselves rather than being influenced by others.
- **Choose to step out of your comfort zones.** Up until now, most of us have had some form of an adult safety net that has kept us nestled within our comfort zones. The world, however, is filled with unique people and opportunities and we can choose to expand our perspectives and open ourselves up to success by simply taking healthy risks.
- **Ask for help.** Help is not finite, and just because we're now adults, doesn't mean that we can't tap into our networks, ask for advice, and gain wisdom. Part of being a responsible adult is understanding that life is a journey of continuous learning. Ask for help when needed, listen to advice when it's given, and then decide what knowledge is applicable.

Smart Money Mindsets to See You Though

For us to take control of our financial future we need to understand that there are three critical components to financial health: management, growth, and protection of our money. Up until this point, spreadsheets and budgets were less intimidating because deviating from the financial goals we set for ourselves only had future consequences. Once we graduate college, *the future becomes right now*, and the bill has finally come due.

Our budget and the financial goals we set for ourselves from here on out will undeniably form part of our financial health but also our overall well-being. And well-being begins with mindset.

For many of us, a lack of exposure to financial literacy and generational ideas of what money is can lead us to develop a poor money mindset. The cold hard reality is that mindset matters in every aspect of our lives, and we need to examine how we think about money and our future before we begin to earn our first real paycheck.

Before we uncover how to develop a healthy money mindset, we must first critically analyze how we currently feel about money. A poor money mindset can be categorized by the following thinking:

- Earning and having money is stressful.
- Managing money is overwhelming.
- Having a job is the only way to make money.
- Holding on to earned money is greed.
- Wealth *should* be distributed.
- Wealth creates more problems than it is worth.

Most of us have some form of poor money mindset that originated from a negative financial experience or cultural or generational ideas. That's why financial literacy is important and why the seven percent works so hard to keep us from achieving a healthy money mindset.

We need to do the work to recognize our money mindsets before it's too late and we solidify these negative beliefs and thoughts by *making poor money decisions.* Every one of us can rewire how we think about money—here's how:

1. **Examine your money emotions.** Do you feel nervous when purchasing a big ticket item, even when you've saved, prepared, and been responsible about the purchase?

Reframe your thoughts and emotions from anxiety to excitement and self-appreciation for the hard work and strategic thought required to make a purchase.

2. **Analyze your thoughts about earnings.** One of the largest obstacles you will face is becoming employed. For a lot of people, a limiting *employee* mindset drives them to believe that they are not successful or cannot earn money unless employed. Entrepreneurship may be a slightly bumpier road when it comes to earning money, but it is a viable option.

3. **Begin to appreciate your earnings capabilities.** I know that many older generations had financial struggles and that you've been told a tale of these hardships at least once. The mistakes past generations made are *not* your mistakes. Be proud of your self-discipline, education, experience, and the financial decisions you've made. You *deserve* to live the life you have crafted for yourself.

4. **Understand your responsibilities.** Lower-income communities have been instilled with a sense of responsibility for their family members and community. While there is nothing wrong with this, it is *not* your responsibility to support others who are making poor financial decisions for themselves—especially if it's at a cost to your emergency savings, retirement fund, paying off student loans, and so on. Yes, creating some room in your budget to support your elders and siblings is noble but you'd be doing far more good teaching them the financial lessons you've learned to become financially healthy.

5. **Let go of selfish narratives:** Consumerism has a darker underbelly than merely enticing you to buy things you don't need—it taps into your capacity to feel guilt. When all other tactics fail, consumerism works to drive guilt. You

can begin to believe that not spending your money on other people is a selfish act (Johnson, 2023a). Let go of this idea and rid yourself of narratives where you're the villain for choosing your financial health—you're not!

Crafting Our Career Path

Dr. Dennis Kimbro (2013) said, "Service is the price you pay for the space you occupy."

For many of us, the words job and career are used interchangeably. A job is employment whereas a career is our chosen career or occupation and is what we will do for most of our adult lives. Have you ever noticed that all of the education you received up to this point was configured so that you could have a high percentage chance of landing a job? What if you wanted to start a business or become an entrepreneur? Where is the education for that? Well if we go back to the concepts of capitalism and consumerism, it becomes clear why there is no financial education to help you become an entrepreneur.

If we just receive a high school diploma, we might be in a position to gain a competitive hourly position at a job. In other words, the job will require clocking in and out in order to get paid for the time rendered for work, no more, no less. If we receive a college degree, we might be in a position to receive a competitive salary position at a job. So, what we are paid is not dependent strictly on time rendered for work, but also a tiny amount of paid vacation and sick leave; however, the responsibilities associated with the job are more demanding, and ultimately more than 40 hours per week will be necessary to meet the requirements. Forget advanced degrees like a Ph.D., J.D., or M.D.—even more time is required. How many hours do you have in a week? Where is the balance? All of this just to work for somebody else. *Hmmm*, how is that so advantageous for us?

So, let's talk about the missing piece of becoming an entrepreneur.

Crafting a career path goes beyond employment or a job. It's the blueprint and the goals we set for our future career success that may include working for certain companies, positions or titles we may want to achieve, entrepreneurship, networking, or business ownership.

Before we create this career blueprint, we need to establish our value so that we know what we are exchanging for our place in an organization or as a business owner. Remember, money is nothing but a tool of trade that helps us to achieve our goals, and in terms of our careers, we are trading our skills and unique value.

Career Goal Setting

Specific, measurable, achievable, realistic, and timely (SMART) goals are shown to be the more effective way of not only setting but achieving our personal and professional goals. Having said that when it comes to our careers, two additional steps are required for a fulfilling career future—empowering and review-able. Let's break SMARTER goals down so that they're specific to career goal setting.

- **Specific:** Set goals that are clear and free of ambiguity.
- **Measurable:** Ensure you are defining how you will measure achievement.
- **Achievable:** Set goals that you can achieve. Lofty goals are healthy, but unachievable goals are not.
- **Realistic:** Be reasonable with what you can attain in your goal time frames.

- **Timely:** Set time-measured milestones for each of your goals.
- **Empowering:** Ensure your goals align with your values and what feels right for you. *Always* remember, your goals are your own.
- **Reviewable:** Goals are not set in stone, especially in the early phases of your career. What matters to you now may not in a year. Market conditions are changeable and you need to develop agility by actively reviewing your goals.

The Job Search Game

Job searching is confusing stuff. We can become defeated, frustrated, and overwhelmed by the sheer number of applications we need to submit to be asked for an interview. As with most other aspects of our adult life, for us to remain focused and productive in our search, we need to be properly prepared.

The steps above will help to narrow down our focus so that we can apply for jobs that match our specific career path criterion. Having said that, some other readiness aspects need to be considered:

- **Documentation:** Job applications require some critical documentation for us to be considered for a position. Ideally, this documentation should be customized to reflect personality. They include a resume, cover letter, and any references of employment and character.
- **Research:** Job searches are deeply personal. Of course, it's important to know what career is being pursued but sometimes we can neglect to take into account our values. A foot in the door is always a good thing, but not considering values can lead to job hopping, which is not a

great reflection on any resume. Instead of applying for everything that fits technical criteria, create a wish list of organizations that would be an ideal fit and apply to these first.

- **Networking:** Searching for employment goes beyond simply looking for a way to make money—it's about relationship building and making a lasting impression. Getting to know others in our chosen industry, remaining polite (even in the face of rejection), and expanding social networks can all prove to be incredibly valuable when looking for a job. Proper connections and relationships present opportunities that often aren't advertised.
- **Consider internships:** Most internships are low-paying or even nonpaying but they offer a window of opportunity to showcase knowledge and skills. For freshly graduated young adults who have little or no working experience, internships are often one of the only ways to break into the job market and prove their value.

Introspective Questions to Ask When Job Searching

- What qualifications and skills are most important to demonstrate?
- What are the most important aspects of myself I want to present?
- What interesting aspects of this industry do I know?
- What additional knowledge and skills would be needed if I were called to interview?
- After researching, does this organization still align with my values and expectations?
- Is there anyone connected to this industry that can introduce me to a network?

- Outside of networking, where are less obvious places I could be presented with employment opportunities?
- What is my hiring timeline?
- Can I afford to search for low-paying or nonpaying internships right now?
- What are my alternatives outside of my chosen industry?

Entrepreneurship as Employment

Modern capitalism-driven industries have changed the face of employment. Gone are the days when employees had a goal of earning a "gold watch" retirement gift, and most modern Americans will change jobs 12 times throughout their careers. Most Americans will change careers five to seven times throughout their working life (Zippia, 2023).

After reading these statistics, it's not surprising that many young graduates choose to take the road less traveled, opting for entrepreneurship as a viable way to make money. Now, becoming a business owner comes with its risks, but for many young adults, the benefits far outweigh the risks taken. Added to these benefits, one of the pros of modern capitalism is the scope for business.

The benefits of entrepreneurship include

- the freedom and independence to decide work hours, the scope of responsibilities and duties, and business development and growth. In essence, entrepreneurs are masters of their ship.
- aligning values directly with employment from the outset. No company is absolutely ideal because they have been built on someone else's values. Owning a business removes personal values, compromises, and disparities.

- making a direct difference through innovation. For young adults who are aware of consumerism tactics, entrepreneurship allows for growth and fresh perspectives in the marketplace.
- hands-on experience that pays more than unpaid internships. Ironically, business ownership is seen as a highly marketable skill in the job market. Owning a business provides you with the experience needed to enter into the job space at a later stage (if you want to), and a good business model will pay from the get-go.
- diversification of income through multiple sources. While owning a business isn't necessarily the most stable income in the early phases, the opportunity to diversify income and gain money from multiple sources makes entrepreneurship a very attractive option.
- natural networking opportunities that employment doesn't offer. Business owners need to deal with suppliers, investors, staff, and customers daily. These interactions allow for a more natural professional network to form and expand opportunities as a direct result.

Starting a business is not much different from conventional job hunting. Goal setting, documentation, and even an internship in the form of shadowing are all still required for a business to be successful.

Government Contracting

Government contracting presents a compelling avenue for entrepreneurs seeking a reliable and lucrative career path for several reasons. First, the government is a consistent and significant buyer, offering a steady stream of opportunities across various industries and sectors, providing stability and predictability for businesses.

Second, government contracts often come with long-term agreements and stable funding, providing entrepreneurs with a reliable source of revenue and the potential for sustained growth.

Third, many government contracts prioritize small and minority-owned businesses through set-aside programs, enabling entrepreneurs to compete on a more level playing field and access opportunities that may be less saturated compared to private sector markets.

These categories provide opportunities for these businesses to compete for contracts without facing direct competition from open-source companies such as Boeing, Oracle, and Lockheed Martin. Overall, government contracting offers entrepreneurs the chance to build a sustainable business, tap into a diverse range of opportunities, and contribute to the public sector while pursuing their career goals. These various governmental contract categories are designed to promote diversity and inclusion in the procurement processes. Here's an overview of some of the key categories:

- **8(a) Contracts:** The 8(a) Business Development program is designed to assist small, disadvantaged businesses, including those owned by minorities and economically disadvantaged individuals. These contracts are set aside exclusively for firms participating in the 8(a) program, allowing them to compete for federal contracts on a more level playing field. Keep in mind that once a company has participated in the program for 8 years, the company is considered an 8a "graduate" and, within two years, has to compete in the open-source market.
- **HUBZone Contracts:** The Historically Underutilized Business Zones (HUBZone) program aims to stimulate economic development in historically underutilized areas by providing federal contracting preferences to small

businesses located in these zones. These contracts are reserved for businesses located in designated HUBZone areas.

- **Women-Owned Small Business (WOSB) Contracts:** The WOSB Federal Contracting program provides contracting opportunities for small businesses owned by women. To qualify, the business must be at least 51% owned and controlled by one or more women. Contracts under this program are set aside for eligible women-owned businesses in industries where women are underrepresented.
- **Service-Disabled Veteran-Owned Small Business (SDVOSB) Contracts:** The SDVOSB program provides procurement opportunities for small businesses owned and controlled by service-disabled veterans. To qualify, the business must be at least 51% owned by one or more service-disabled veterans. Contracts set aside for SDVOSBs provide opportunities for disabled veterans to participate in federal contracting.
- **Minority-Owned Business Contracts:** While there isn't a specific federal program exclusively for minority-owned businesses, certain contracts may be set aside for businesses owned by minorities if they meet the criteria for other programs like 8(a) or SDVOSB.
- **Small Disadvantaged Business (SDB) Contracts:** Small Disadvantaged Businesses may also qualify for contracts under various federal agencies' SDB programs. These programs aim to ensure that small businesses owned by socially and economically disadvantaged individuals have fair access to federal contracting opportunities.
- **Veteran-Owned Small Business (VOSB) Contracts:** While not exclusive to disabled veterans, the VOSB program provides procurement opportunities for small

businesses owned and controlled by veterans. To qualify, the business must be at least 51% owned by one or more veterans.

These categories provide minority and small businesses with avenues to compete for federal contracts without direct competition from open-source companies, thereby promoting diversity and inclusion in government procurement. Businesses interested in pursuing these opportunities should familiarize themselves with the specific eligibility requirements and certification processes for each program.

Additionally, they should actively monitor contracting opportunities on platforms like the System for Award Management (SAM) at sam.gov and engage in networking and outreach activities within the federal contracting community to enhance their chances of success.

The First Paycheck and Beyond

The first paycheck as a graduated adult is exciting and, dare I say, tempting. Until now, our budgets were focused on saving when we were younger, and living modestly as we moved through college. Because most jobs have some form of probationary period attached to them, I would suggest that we continue to live a college-oriented frugal lifestyle until a job is secured.

This will allow for additional amounts to be saved and placed into our college capital loan amount. Having said that, we do need to adequately prepare and budget for our new earnings, tweaking our budget so that we don't fall straight back into consumer spending traps.

With our larger earnings, we can now look at reintroducing some "nicer" to have needs spending costs and reevaluate our other expenses so that they align with our renewed career and life goals. The 50-30-20 rule still applies now, but expenses like rent and insurance may increase as we make big-ticket purchases. In addition, at this stage of our lives, we may want to consider investing and may need to adjust our budget percentages accordingly.

Understanding Employee Benefits

Employees who are on probation are afforded the same benefits and rights as full-time workers. This means at a minimum, we're entitled to fair pay, statutory paid sick leave, and fundamental employment rights.

Part of these employment rights includes any employee benefits offered through an organization. They can include

- health insurance
- life insurance
- dental insurance
- retirement contribution programs
- flexible spending or health savings accounts
- paid vacation and sick time
- paid holidays
- flexible working hours
- education assistance

As an employee who is on probation, we may only be able to negotiate our benefits once the probationary period has been completed. Some organizations, however, will present an employment offer from the outset.

When an offer is received, we have the right to negotiate benefits but to do so, we need to first understand how negotiations and these benefits will affect our employment. A great way to begin negotiating is to research industry standards, including salary trends, geographic location (where the job is offered), skills, licenses, certifications, and years of experience in the role. Salary data is freely available on the internet and sites like Indeed offer a free personal calculator that helps work out an average for the position applied for. Once we know what to expect, we can formulate a discussion around salary and benefits.

Always remember that benefits are not a given. There are plenty of people in the marketplace who aren't afforded the privilege of negotiating salaries or benefits. Lead with gratitude and understand that the organization is investing time and money into the hiring process.

Balancing Work With Life

When it comes to creating balance between work and your personal life, Zig Zigler had this to say, "Success is not about climbing up the ladder of your career at the expense of your personal life. It's about finding the harmony between the two, where one enhances the other, and together, they create a fulfilling life."

Striving for a work-life balance is more than guru nonsense, it's an essential skill that we need to learn as we begin working for a full-time paycheck. It's easy to become wrapped up in our work as a way to prove our value in an organization but not prioritizing balance is counterproductive.

We need to understand that work is a means to an end—a way to achieve our goals—but also something to be grateful for. If we are happy to simply do our job and fill our time outside of work with whatever interests us, chances are we're not going to achieve our career goals. We need to show gratitude for the position we're in and accept that work, in itself, is a meaningful pursuit of our growth and development.

Like our other pursuits in life, there is a time and a space for the milestones and responsibilities required for success. With that in mind, I'm not denying that passion and purpose-driven employment is a privilege. It may take time to find a company that ideally aligns with our goals and passions in life. Sometimes we need to compromise so that we can achieve what we set out for our lives.

Finally, understand that a work-life balance sometimes isn't possible. Life requires us to be adaptable to our circumstances. Sometimes we'll need to dedicate more energy to work, other times our personal lives will require more of our attention. Balance is not a definitive extreme, it's finding the middle ground and choosing to consciously remain in this space.

The Financial Future: Planning Ahead

Graduating college and finding full-time employment or starting a business doesn't automatically guarantee financial independence. For many of us, prioritizing paying off student loans, fine-tuning our budgets, and remaining within the safer confines of a college lifestyle is preferred for the first couple of years out of college.

We need to be mindful of the fact that consumerism and capitalism are usually most prevalent during critical junctures of our lives. We're indoctrinated to believe that once we have a full-time job, our lives need to change to fit our paycheck. The pressure to buy a new car, upscale our living arrangements, and upgrade our furniture becomes particularly overwhelming as a new graduate.

Yes, it's great to have goals in mind, but placing financial pressure on ourselves to achieve financial independence at this early age is unrealistic, especially with the exorbitant cost of living we're facing. Instead, we should take the time to pencil in our new adult goals, assess our income and daily expenses, and prioritize a more practical approach to achieving our overarching goals.

Financial independence can *never* be achieved by submitting to *consumer ideals* of what the next steps of our lives *should* look like. Instead of placing focus on all of the *shoulds*, we must find a balance, employ all of the knowledge we've learned, and be steadfast in pursuing our long-term financial goals.

As we challenge ourselves to tick off one milestone at a time, the short-term goals of purchasing a new vehicle, investing, moving into a bigger home, starting a family, and so on will automatically be achieved. In planning, we should only focus on the "what" and not worry about the "how." Let the "how" take care of itself in the supernatural realm. What I learned is that planning gives us the confidence and wisdom to face the unknown. That within itself may be scary because we don't have much control over it, but I am not denying that the future is scary.

I have succeeded and failed miserably in creating my career plan at the same time. But the opposite of success is not failure. The opposite of success is conforming to the way it is in the moment and quitting before it changes. You are grown now, a certified adult. Don't quit no matter how much adversity comes your way!

Personal Finance Highlights

Preparing for life after college is indeed a daunting yet exciting journey filled with endless possibilities. By embracing realistic expectations, intentional living, risk-taking, seeking support, and financial empowerment, young adults can confidently navigate this transition period and embark on a path toward personal and professional fulfillment. Remember, success is not just about reaching the destination but also about embracing the journey with courage, resilience, and determination.

1. Navigating the Transition to Adulthood: Graduating from college marks a significant transition into adulthood, where the responsibilities of finding employment, managing finances, and establishing a career path become real. It's a time of both excitement and trepidation as young adults face the challenges of the job market and financial independence.

2. Embracing Resilience and Intentional Living: Success doesn't come overnight, and it's essential to instill in young adults the value of resilience and intentional living. By setting clear goals, making deliberate decisions, and embracing healthy risks, they can navigate the complexities of adulthood with confidence and purpose.

3. Developing a Healthy Money Mindset: Understanding the importance of financial literacy and cultivating a healthy money mindset is crucial for long-term financial well-being. By reframing negative beliefs about money, appreciating earnings capabilities, and taking control of financial responsibilities, young adults can lay the foundation for a secure financial future.

4. Crafting a Career Blueprint: Transitioning from employment to entrepreneurship offers a unique opportunity for young adults to take control of their careers. By setting SMARTER goals, exploring entrepreneurial ventures, and leveraging networking opportunities, they can create a fulfilling career path that aligns with their values and aspirations.

5. Seeking Support and Continuous Learning: Asking for help and seeking guidance from mentors, peers, and professionals is a sign of strength, not weakness. Young

adults should tap into their networks, ask for advice, and embrace opportunities for continuous learning and personal development. By seeking support and learning from others' experiences, they can navigate challenges more effectively and make informed decisions about their future.

CHAPTER 11
CONQUERING THE FEAR
OF THE FUTURE

O ne of the biggest lessons I learned with my kids was that being a parent doesn't end once they're grown. Sure, the role changes—we shift from educator and guardian to safe space and mentor, but on some level, our children will always need us.

Being a parent to an adult can be tricky territory. We need to continue to guide and mentor our children through the maze of adulthood while ensuring we don't enable negative behaviors. Shielding adult children too much can result in a lack of responsibility and them being ill-equipped to deal with life. Taking a "you're on your own now," stance can lead to burnout, poor decision-making, and mental health issues.

We need to strike a balance between being a safe, open space for our kids to bounce ideas off of, offering guidance when asked, and setting boundaries for unacceptable behavior. We also need to be aware that the world is a very different place. In the 1970s and 1980s, unemployment was pegged in the lower to mid-single digits, with 1983 being the only year job availability reached lower double digits.

After a renewed recession, unemployment is still recovering from double-digit figures. Even more alarming, job uncertainty, layoffs, and a preference for those who are prepared to work for the bare minimum wage mean having a job is no longer the safety net it once was (U.S. Bureau of Labor Statistics, 2024).

Our kids are facing a world that is not only driven by a consumerism-capitalism hybrid but also a place of deep employment and financial uncertainty and it's up to us to help them navigate and overcome their understandable fear of the future.

Understanding the Fear of the Future

Research shows that no daily concern affects Americans more than financial anxiety. A study conducted in 2022 showed that 87% of people reported inflation and job uncertainty as the primary cause of their stress and anxiety and for good reason (American Psychological Association, 2022).

The fear of meeting our financial needs and commitments and undoing all of the smart work we put in during our younger years can be overwhelming. Now, before continuing with this chapter, I'd like to acknowledge that we can't always fix the number in our bank account, but we can take steps to manage money-related anxiety and plan properly.

Recognizing Financial Anxiety

Some level of financial anxiety is good. It drives us to make healthy financial decisions for ourselves and ensure we remain on track with our goals. For some of us, financial anxiety can be crippling and can stem from our financial history, low income, rising costs of living, financial overcommitment, or debt.

Some symptoms of financial anxiety include

- feeling sick when dealing with finances or checking bank balances
- avoiding bills
- becoming stuck in decision loops
- poor work-life balance
- rigid financial thinking
- ruminating money thoughts
- trouble sleeping

Ignoring financial anxiety is counterproductive and can lead to everything from hoarding tendencies to gambling, addiction, over-spending, and depression. The psychological and physiological impacts of financial stress and anxiety cannot be downplayed and while it may feel easier to hide from our financial realities, we must face our fears head-on to secure our financial future.

The Path to Financial Security

Nothing in life is certain. We can plan, prepare, and practice good habits to mitigate the risk of financial setbacks, but we cannot predict whether we will suffer one or more financial challenges.

The road between now and the future may be paved with some uncertainty but we can bridge this gap. The first anchor is financial confidence through education.

- **Educate yourself in finance.** We cannot make wise decisions for ourselves if we do not first know what options are available to us, what is happening in the economy, or how the marketplace is pivoting and changing. Make financial knowledge and wisdom an ongoing commitment so that you can stay ahead of trends and manipulation tactics.

- **Commit to action.** Even the best-laid plans will not come to anything if we don't commit and take action. It's never too late to start creating a financially free future for yourself. I've met people who started investing and saving in their 40s and it had a positive effect in their 70s.
- **Savings are important.** Saving in different ways is incredibly important throughout the different phases of our lives. A good starting goal as we enter adulthood is to save 20% of our salary, dividing this amount equally between savings and investments. If more can be spared without affecting needs expenses, we should consider saving more rather than increasing wants spending.
- **Think about career breaks.** There are very few people who know when a recession or dip in the job marketplace will occur. A good way to build confidence is to consider how long we could go without a salary before having to dip into our savings and investments. Once we know how much this amount is, we can begin to work toward setting aside a separate saved amount to cover unforeseen layoffs.
- **Find someone financially savvy.** The best advice received is gained from real-life experience. Speaking with someone who has experienced financial setbacks, overcome hardships, and is financially resilient is a good way to gain both advice and confidence.
- **Know a skill's value.** While most of us are new in our industries now, a proper career plan and skills development will inevitably increase our worth. Knowing our value allows us to negotiate our pay and potential raises when the time is right.

Overcoming Financial Challenges: Building Financial Resilience

We now know that the key to overcoming financial challenges is to formulate a proper strategy that allows us to deal with each unique challenge individually. At the top of this list is financial education and creating financial buffers that can help us weather income shortages, but what about unexpected expenses?

Recent statistics show that more than 40% of Americans are unprepared for an emergency expense of over $1,000 (Gillespie, 2023). That's nearly half of the adult population that would be completely derailed if they were hit by a financial crisis!

Granted, at this age, a large, unexpected expense is not ideal, but there are ways of overcoming this without dipping too much into our savings.

- **Reduce expenses.** Revisiting budgets and making the necessary lifestyle adjustments for a short period can help cut down on expenses dramatically. Any money saved from cutting back on expenses can be used to recover from a loss and replenish any savings used.
- **Temporarily increase earnings.** Look at ways to earn extra income and diversify income streams. Extra money earned can be used to defray costs as well as pay off debt incurred from a financial setback.
- **Consider smart credit.** While it can be tempting to use a credit card in times of financial crisis, the interest charged can often lead us into deep financial debt. If our credit score allows, it may be a better idea to look at applying for a personal loan with much lower interest. Always keep in mind that minimum payments must be affordable, and we

should not borrow more than what is needed, no matter how tempting a credit offer is.

A Word on Credit Card Use in Times of Financial Crisis

Sometimes, we have no choice but to use our credit cards. When this becomes the case, it's imperative to do so with wisdom so that we can maximize savings and minimize debt incurred.

- Ensure the card being used has the lowest possible interest rate and if possible, no fees.
- Enquire about cash-back offers that can earn money on essential purchases. While this percentage is usually low, every dollar counts when suffering a setback.
- If possible, enquire about rewards programs that are meaningful to the current situation. For example, some organizations are aligned with grocery stores and may offer discounts on food.
- Think outside the box when it comes to rewards. While accumulating Amazon credits, for example, may not seem helpful, they can be used to purchase pantry food items.
- One of the biggest issues with using a credit card to cover needs expenses is that it becomes very difficult to dig ourselves out of debt. Always look for alternatives to financing big issues other than credit cards including emergency funds. However, resist the temptation to dip into your savings or the "Golden Goose." That money is set aside to work for you long-term with compound interest. Leave that money alone at all costs!

The Psychology of Financial Confidence

To build financial confidence, we need to have a solid plan and we also need to overcome our limiting beliefs and biases. Having an achievable plan, an ideal in mind, and defining success are all great but we must always be aware of our ability to subconsciously sabotage ourselves. Overcome this temptation and succeed anyway. Remember, we may have to fail our way to success.

For us to become truly financially confident we need to examine our mindset so that we can move from a space of "enough" to a space that capitalism doesn't want us to reside—abundance!

Kathryn Hanna (2022) said, "Confidence in my ability to achieve clear financial goals was the key turning point, not the achievement of any set amount of wealth." While this quote might seem contradictory, the answer to abundance and financial confidence lies in our ability to remove whatever capitalist concept of wealth we may have.

Let me ask you directly—what defines wealth? A million dollars, fifty million dollars, a billion dollars? Wealth, like success, has no definition, and specifying any amount of what we deem enough money limits us in not only making money but in growing money wisely. Now, before I continue, setting financial goals is not setting limitations because goals are malleable. Once we achieve a goal, we should be formulating a new one to help us grow further. Placing a cap on what we want to achieve, however, is limiting, and has been instilled in us by the capitalist-consumerism hybrid that governs our thought processes and keeps us financially illiterate.

Shedding Bias and Limiting Beliefs

A consumer mindset is driven by fear and scarcity. When affected by consumer bias, our financial decisions are driven by a belief that there will never be enough and that the way to happiness is through acquisition and consumption. Consumerism not only feeds a financial scarcity mindset but also taps into our subconscious biases, driving us to make decisions based on whatever limitations we've set for ourselves.

Consumerism is the Chinese finger trap of financial entrapment, and to liberate ourselves from its grips, we need to work on uncovering our self-limiting beliefs and changing our mindsets.

Before we can overcome anything we must first recognize it's a problem. Use mindfulness, jot down thoughts about money, and ask others to examine your "money language" for subtle cues to your biases. For example, I had a friend who no matter how much money they had, would declare, "I don't have money for that," every time something unexpected came up. This statement was a clear indicator of their loss aversion bias which caused them to be financially careless.

Once a bias is uncovered, we must challenge the belief, presenting facts so that we can untangle consumer ideas and unhealthy thoughts we may have about money. When we catch ourselves acting in a certain way, we should curiously examine our behaviors, questioning why we think or behave the way we do.

Questioning a belief allows us to create a robust plan to overcome ingrained behaviors. A great way to do this is to go back and review financial goals to uncover limitations we've placed on ourselves because of a challenged belief or bias.

Finally, we can begin to cultivate the money mindset we want, free from self-limiting beliefs. On some level, we will always uncover new biases that have been instilled in us but by cultivating a money mindset of confidence and abundance, we can more easily recognize where we are limiting ourselves. Once we realize our limiting beliefs are mere illusions, we can then tap into our unlimited potential where our worth is only dependent on how much of the globe our value will reach. And yes, your value will be rewarded.

Financial Independence and Career Choices/Long-Term Security

Entering the job market opens new opportunities for us but it also begins to shift our focus from short- and mid-term goals to long-term ones. At this stage, we may begin to think about creating a family, supporting our immediate family, or our retirement. A comfortable retirement until this point has been reserved for savings and safe investments.

As our careers evolve, however, we must start prioritizing retirement and generational wealth. Having a financial plan not only ensures we build strong habits to overcome consumerism but also helps us seize opportunities for financial growth and establish a strong foundation for future generations within our generational line. Below is a list of key actions that set us up for a comfortable retirement.

- Begin saving and stay committed.
- Build an emergency fund.
- Actively negotiate a job with retirement benefits.
- Set up an automatic saving facility (pay yourself first).
- Match your 401(k).
- Expand on strategic investments.
- Avoid accumulating debt.
- If eligible, claim the saver's credit.

While we may have the choice to make riskier investments at this age, I don't suggest this. Instead, I choose to diversify investments so that risk and return are balanced. For pure retirement savings that aren't independently invested, opt for the safest possible option that will maximize return and mitigate risk.

Legacy and Generational Wealth

On generational wealth, Beyonce (2018) had this to say, "My great-great-grandchildren already rich. That's a lot of brown 'chi'r'en' on your Forbes list."

Generational wealth is the financial legacy we pass on to the generation after us. This could be our children, siblings, sibling's children, and so on. Generational wealth is sometimes referred to as family or legacy wealth.

This wealth is passed on in the form of inheritance which can be a mix of assets, possessions, investments, savings, and retirement benefits (if beneficiaries are properly listed). What we must not neglect when it comes to leaving behind a legacy is the financial education and literacy we have learned so that future generations can continue to have financial freedom. There are several ways we can build generational wealth, including

- investing in the stock market
- investing in maintained real estate
- building a business that can be inherited or sold
- investing in life insurance
- creating a college or education fund
- diversifying income streams
- ensuring debt is paid off
- creating a solid estate plan
- committing to continued financial literacy and education

Creating an Estate Plan

Having an estate plan is critical to transferring wealth. We must understand that the larger an estate is, the more complicated it can get, so having a solid plan in place is an absolute must. I recommend consulting an attorney when creating this plan and reviewing it often as wealth, assets, and additional goals are achieved.

When planning an estate's division, we need to

- **Set up a revocable living trust.** This is the center of your estate plan. All other businesses, rental properties, personal valuables, and future ambitions should be listed, owned, and managed by the living trust under your name.
- **Create a will.** Regardless of whether an estate plan is in place, a will is critical. Wills must concisely outline our exact wishes for our accumulated wealth. It should be embedded within your revocable living trust, but a stand-alone will is better than nothing.
- **Set up custodial accounts.** Set up custodial accounts preferably in the form of irrevocable trusts for minors of your choosing. Whereas custodial accounts are accessible once the minor turns 18, irrevocable trusts give additional stipulations on conditions where the trust will be awarded such as requirements to go to college and maintain a certain GPA. Irrevocable trusts give specific instructions on how to award the beneficiary by the executor and the requirements that must be met. However, once the irrevocable trust is executed, unlike a revocable trust, it can no longer be controlled or revoked.

In addition, setting up a revocable living trust with the will embedded within the trust ensures matters are not handed to the probate courts, which have an 18-month wait time for a possible misinterpretation of how to distribute your assets. Keep in mind that a will is only enacted once we pass away. A revocable living trust also gives governing doctrine to execute in the case that you go into an extended coma or a state where you are unable to render any kind of financial decisions.

Right now, life is getting real. It's time to buy assets and things that will help us build a financial future for our family and we need to establish the most efficient and effective way to do this.

Personal Finance Highlights

In essence, by embracing the responsibilities of parenting in adult-hood, confronting financial anxieties, overcoming challenges, shedding limiting beliefs, and building generational wealth, we empower ourselves and future generations to navigate life's uncertainties with confidence and resilience. It's time to take charge of our financial future and build a legacy that extends beyond ourselves.

1. Parenting in Adulthood: The role of a parent extends far beyond childhood. As our children navigate adulthood, we transition from being their guardians to becoming mentors and safe spaces. Striking a balance between offering guidance and setting boundaries is crucial in supporting them through life's challenges.

2. Financial Anxiety Is Real, But Manageable: In today's uncertain economic climate, financial anxiety is a prevalent concern. Acknowledging and addressing this anxiety is the first step towards financial well-being. By educating ourselves about personal finance and taking proactive steps to manage money-related stress, we can regain control of our financial future.

3. Building Financial Resilience Through Education and Action: Financial security is not guaranteed, but it can be cultivated through continuous learning and proactive decision-making. By committing to ongoing financial education, taking action towards savings and investments, and preparing for unforeseen challenges such as career breaks, we can enhance our financial resilience.

4. Shedding Bias and Limiting Beliefs: Consumerism perpetuates fear and scarcity, influencing our financial decisions. By recognizing and challenging our limiting beliefs, we can cultivate a mindset of abundance and financial confidence, allowing us to pursue our goals without self-imposed limitations.

5. Building Generational Wealth: Planning for retirement and establishing a solid estate plan are essential steps toward creating generational wealth. By diversifying investments, prioritizing financial literacy, and setting up custodial accounts or trusts, we can ensure a secure financial future for ourselves and our descendants.

CHAPTER 12
SAVING FOR MILESTONES, 1ST CAR, 1ST HOUSE, AND FAMILY

Most of us remember our first big purchases and the milestones of adulthood but what we tend to forget is the sheer overwhelm, and sometimes analysis paralysis, that accompanies these milestones.

As our adult children approach 30, most will begin to consider purchasing big-ticket items, like a house or new car, and some will start creating families of their own. Their focus shifts from immediate short-term goals to mid- and long-term goals that demand sound decision-making.

It is also at this point that our role as parents shifts into mentorship and assisting our adult children in making the right choices for them. We must set aside our hang-ups and biases so that we can listen with the intent of understanding our children's concerns.

We must also acknowledge that big-ticket purchases, especially home ownership, have become a real issue for young adults. Statistics suggest that a combination of corporate buyouts that have caused a bidding war, higher home prices, and elevated housing repayments mean that home ownership is impossible for most young adults (Edwards, 2023). Our kids are being forced into a rental market that is dominated by corporate landlords who are backed by huge private equity groups. Prices of domestic properties have increased astronomically since 2021 and young adults are being squeezed out of the housing market because of capitalist greed.

The Road to Financial Milestones

Today's young adults are battling several obstacles that older adults don't need to. From rampant consumerism to rising home prices and the exorbitant cost of college tuition, Millennials, Gen Z, and Gen Alphas need to be savvier with the financial decisions they make for themselves.

While formulating a financial roadmap that includes big milestone purchases like a new car or home is important, we do need to acknowledge any limitations we may face and ensure we're not setting ourselves back for the sake of what consumerism says we should have achieved.

Comparing ourselves to our parents or those entering the job and housing market is pointless. Between 1980 and 2021, the housing market has increased by more than 200%, the availability of housing has decreased, and young adults are entering the job market later because more of us are attending college to finish degree programs.

It's not, however, all doom and gloom, and we can plan appropriately to reach the adult milestones we would like to achieve by tying our career goals in with our financial milestones. The way to do this is to shift our focus from society-driven young adult expectations and rather focus on future-based financial freedom goals.

These include

- securing your first career-building position
- funding emergency savings
- beginning a retirement plan
- investing in assets and commodities
- paying off credit card and personal loan debt
- paying off student loan debt

Once we have achieved these milestones, we should have enough liquidity to consider big-ticket purchases like a home.

Home Ownership and Real Estate

There is a current real estate war going on that is squeezing the first-time homebuyer out of the market. The demand for single-family homes outweighs the supply because most homeowners are not selling like they were over a decade ago. Homeownership has been considered the staple for financial success in the US for so many years, but now it feels like it is getting too expensive for the average first-time buyer to adequately engage. This is disconcerting for me.

We need to pay closer attention to homeownership as a financial goal by examining the current real estate situation so that we can better manage our expectations of buying a home.

The housing market may be headed for a bubble again because some property owners are using the equities on their homes to further obtain loans. The denial of affordable access to homeownership is now gradually shifting the American dream of home ownership to other areas of interest, like business ownership.

While all of the above factors may lead to a drop in the demand for homes in the short run, in the long run, the housing market will crash as the bubble bursts leaving people with exorbitant mortgages they cannot afford and homes that cannot be sold for what is owed.

Those who are willing to play the long game, waiting for the value of housing to drop, will benefit from lower prices and increased "stock." This, of course, doesn't mean we cannot consider home-ownership now—it simply means ensuring we have considered all possibilities for our financial security.

If owning a home is clearly our ticket to proving that we have arrived at adulthood, I would recommend the following steps:

1. Instead of a single-family home, try to purchase a duplex if you are investing on your own.
2. Network with colleagues moving to the same area who are willing to partner with you and invest collectively.
3. Purchase a multifamily unit or an apartment complex as a limited liability company (LLC). That way each of you can occupy a unit and rent out the remaining units. This cuts your mortgage down by 50% or more while drawing income in the process.
4. Once occupancy is full for 1–2 years, plan to move out of your unit using a down payment saved from collected rent.
5. Fill in the occupancy of the apartment with full rent capacity rendering more income.
6. Close on your first single-family home.

The Path to Home Ownership

Owning a home requires several steps, especially if we are funding this home with a mortgage. Understanding both the terminology and options available to us when purchasing a home will ensure we are making wise financial decisions for ourselves and mitigating additional costs that may be lying in wait for us.

We begin this understanding by assessing the costs required to purchase a home outside of our mortgage repayments.

- **Lender fees:** When buying a house using credit facilities like mortgages or FHA loans, origination fees are charged. These fees can be between one and two percent of the home's price.
- **Appraiser fees:** The price of a property needs to be assessed against the market value of other similar homes in the intended purchase area. An appraiser is used to assess this price and a fee needs to be paid for the appraiser's service and skills.
- **Real estate attorney fees:** Contracting documents, tax, financial and legal liabilities, change of ownership, and a range of other legal factors will need to be attended to by an attorney. As with appraisers, a fee needs to be paid for these specialized skills.
- **Title search and insurance fees:** This is a necessary part of buying a home to ensure that there are no title defects. The change of name on the title, as well as insurance on the property, are charged as a fee.
- **Building inspection fees:** While not a compulsory fee, it's recommended that an inspection is done on the condition of a home to detect any potential major structural issues that can affect us in the future.

We can expect to pay between two and five percent of a home's value in fees. This is in addition to a down payment, mortgage payments, moving costs, and any renovation and decoration plans we may have.

Monthly homeownership costs depend on how a purchase is funded (type of mortgage, down payment size, tax benefits, and so on). The most common of these costs, however, are

- monthly mortgage repayment including interest
- any maintenance and repair needed
- homeowners insurance
- property taxes

Statistics show that the average mortgage payment on a 30-year fixed mortgage in 2024 is $2,833 per month and $3,749 on a 15-year fixed mortgage without additional cost considerations (Knueven & Grace, 2024).

Saving for a Down Payment

Saving for a down payment is a critical step in securing a mortgage. Some mortgage options require a substantial down payment, while other lending options may require a smaller down payment based on several requirements, including credit history, the number of current loans payable, liquidity, assets, and so on.

Saving for a down payment can feel overwhelming, especially in today's economic environment but there are ways to accumulate savings for our first home.

- **Use certificate of deposits (CDs).** These have slightly higher compound interest than the regular compound interest rate of savings accounts. If saving for a short, specified amount of time, CDs are a great way to accumulate for down payments.

- **Take advantage of extra money-generating opportunities.** Performance bonuses, tax deductions, cost-saving measures, and any other way to bring in extra cash can be diverted to CDs or a money market account to increase savings temporarily.
- **Put certain variable expenses on hold.** Certain expenses that have no significant impact on our ability to work or that directly impact our well-being can be diverted to a savings account. This could include gym memberships, streaming services, and so on.
- **Diversify your income.** Short-term side hustles can dramatically increase our savings capabilities not just in the present but in the future. Side hustles help to diversify income streams and additional income can be placed straight into savings.
- **Pay off other loans.** Paying off credit card debt and other loans quickly can create a lot of disposable income. Instead of using these repayment amounts, divert them to your savings account to build your down payment efficiently.

Types of Mortgages

The type of mortgage and amount we can loan are affected by several criteria including our credit history, credit score, down payment, current assets, income, and number of people applying for the loan to name a few.

When assessing our creditworthiness and how much we can afford to lend, the bank will use a formula to work out our debt-to-income ratio (DTI). Different lenders will have varying ways to work our specific DTI out but generally speaking, this is done by adding all monthly debt payments and dividing this number by our income before taxes and other deductions. This number is then expressed as a percentage. Ideally, DTI should be kept below 36% but I would suggest nothing more than 28%. While some lending institutions will still consider offering a mortgage to people with a DTI of under 43%, this is incredibly risky for the buyer's financial health and well-being (Murphy, 2024).

The types of mortgages available to us include

- **Conventional home loans, aka mortgages:** A minimum 20% down payment of the home price is required or a 7% down payment may be accepted with the requirement of paying mortgage insurance until our equity in the home has reached 20%. In addition, a credit score of 620 or more and a DTI of less than 43% is required.
- **Federal Housing Administration (FHA) loans:** Loans offered by the government to first-time home buyers. A down payment of 3.5% of the property value, a minimum credit score of 580, and a DTI ratio of 43% are required to qualify.
- **Veteran Affairs (VA) loans:** Loans offered by the federal government for both active and retired U.S. military personnel and their spouses. No down payment, credit score, or DTI are assessed. Instead, 90 days of active duty service, six years of Reserves or National Guard service (DTI assessed), 181 days of active duty in peacetimes, 90 days of cumulative service under Title 10 or Title 32, or the death of a spouse in the line of duty are used as assessment criteria. Veterans injured and disabled in the line of duty also qualify for VA loans.
- **United States Department of Agriculture (USDA) loans:** The only notable requirement for this loan is that the

property be located in a rural area in the United States. Household income must be below the median salary of the area the property is in. No down payment or credit score is required, however, a DTI of no more than 41% is required.

Navigating the Mortgage Process

Purchasing a home begins by first finding out how much we qualify for and whether or not we can *comfortably* afford the repayments on this amount. This process is called pre-approval and lets us know what our options are before we begin shopping around for houses.

Once we are approved and have the required down payment, we can begin viewing homes that fit within our budget, *not the pre-approved* amount. Remember, just because we qualify for a larger loan doesn't mean we *should* use this full amount.

After agreeing on a property price with the seller, we can begin the mortgage process by providing our chosen lending provider with information like

- employment details
- detailed annual income by presenting W-2 forms for the last two years
- listing and proving other assets
- declaring all debt including alimony and child support
- supplying the proposed property's information
- disclosing all credit information including collections, bankruptcies, and delinquencies

This information will be fact-checked and verified, and a loan estimate document will be provided. This document will contain an estimate of how much we can qualify for, down payment requirements, and so on. A loan estimate is valid for 10 business days, allowing us to shop around for better offers from other lending institutions.

After an estimate document is accepted, the underwriting process begins to check and verify the property information. At this stage, appraisals will also be conducted.

Finally, the sale of the property will close once the mortgage is approved. Our newly purchased home will now belong to the mortgagee (lender) until our final payment is made and the property is transferred into our name as sole owners.

Renting vs. Owning a Home

Entering into the housing market is tougher now than it was 10 years ago. The reasons for this have been discussed above, but for those who have done their due diligence, have qualified for and can afford a mortgage, and are still unsure, renting a home can still be tempting.

To quantify the decision we'll make between owning and renting, we must weigh the pros and cons of homeownership versus renting.

Renting a Home

One of the biggest myths consumerism will have us believe is that renters are throwing away their money every month. This isn't true at all because renting responsibly is still fulfilling a basic human need.

Renting may not build equity for us, but it does ensure we're not burdened with the costs of homeownership. Renting provides us with both stability and agility because monthly rent costs are fixed (annual or lease renewal dependent), and we can easily scale up or down where we live according to our affordability requirements. In addition, most costs associated with homeownership, like utilities, storage, and homeowners association fees, are covered by the landlord.

Renters face some uncertainty in modern housing markets and as more corporations purchase homes and apartments, rent increases can be quite steep at renewal time. This can mean renters will *have* to move to find something more affordable. To mitigate fluctuating prices and greedy landlords, we can, however, look for housing that is rent-controlled or house hunt in areas with rent ceilings.

Owning a Home

Homeownership comes with a distinct set of advantages. These include flexibility in the look and feel of the interior of your home, building equity, and a sense of stability in where we live. While the overall cost of homeownership tends to be higher than renting, for some, the stability of owning property and ensuring they have a future asset.

On the downside, homeownership will include hidden costs that many are not prepared for including

- property tax
- water and sewer services
- pest control
- garden maintenance
- insurance
- and several other specialty costs including pool cleaning, flood insurance, and earthquake insurance

Renting vs. Owning at a Glance

Renting a home	Owning a home
The flexibility to move when required.	Provides a sense of stability.
Budget flexibility.	Can help build equity.
Stable monthly repayments.	Allows for creative freedom.
Repairs and maintenance are the landlord's responsibility.	A property can be used to leverage other loans if necessary.
Fair notice is required for price increases or when a property will be sold.	Allows owners to create generational wealth

Purchasing Your First New Vehicle

Buying a new car is another adult first, according to consumerism, but what if I told you that the average age of new car buyers in the US is 52? Or that the average age of cars on the road in the US is 12.5 years (Tucker, 2023)?

Consumerism would have us believe that we need to put ourselves in debt for a car as a sign of status or success and that owning a new vehicle is somehow asset accumulation. The cold, hard reality is that very few vehicles are pure assets; most are depreciating assets, and some are outright liabilities.

A new car loses up to 20% of its value within the first year of ownership and anywhere between 9 and 11% of its value the moment you drive it off the lot. By the fifth year of ownership, a new car will have lost nearly half its value (Bankrate, 2022).

Navigating car loans and repayments is tricky territory and before we blindly purchase a new vehicle just for the sake of it, we should take a moment to assess our needs, affordability aspects, and the future implications of owning a vehicle. Here are some questions to ask ourselves before committing to a new car.

- **What car do I need?** Remember, wants and needs vary drastically, and consumerism targets our wants or desires. To make a wise financial decision, we need to separate wants and needs, homing in on aligning our vehicle with functionality, capabilities, lifestyle, and affordability needs.
- **What are the benefits?** New cars, admittedly, come with certain features that may be cost-saving. These features include improved fuel consumption, stop-start technology, and proximity sensors. Used cars, however, may save immediate money, with dealers cutting prices to clear the previous year's models in August and September of the following year.
- **What are the running expenses?** Monthly costs like insurance, maintenance, repairs, and gas vary based on the age, make, and model of a car. The cost of tires, for example, can vary dramatically, ranging from $100 to $3,000 per tire.
- **What is the car's condition?** Sometimes, new cars are sold at a reduced price because they have been used for test-driving demonstrations. These cars are called demos and come with a less hefty price tag. Demos and used vehicles need to have their condition assessed before committing to a purchase.
- **What is the total cost?** No financed car deal comes free of additional costs. With new cars, these extra fees are added to the total price of the vehicle. When receiving an estimate, it's important to request the total monthly cost

including insurance, seller commission, financing charges, service or maintenance warranties, and so on.

- **What is the availability of parts?** Certain cars will have lower parts costs and higher availability, reducing costs in the long term. Conversely, certain vehicles will have low availability and high parts costs. Unavailability of parts can mean you're without a vehicle or need to pay for another vehicle while you wait, costing you money.

Saving for a Car

After reading the above and taking the time to analyze our financial standings, we may decide that financing a car with a loan simply isn't worth the added monthly expense.

Saving for a car is not much different from other big-ticket purchases and involves

- calculating the full price of the vehicle
- factoring in other expenses like maintenance, service, and insurance costs
- setting monthly savings goals based on the full price of the vehicle and the time you will save
- making adjustments to your budget, paying off credit card debt, and freeing up money that can be directed to a savings account
- setting up automatic savings transfers to prevent accidental spending
- taking on a side hustle to increase earnings temporarily

Teaching Kids About Money

For some of us, approaching 30 comes with a new milestone, one that is more life-changing than any other: having kids of our own.

We cannot expect that the government or schools will teach our kids financial literacy. The wheels of change are often slow and can come to a grinding halt when funded by those driving consumerism.

We must equip our kids with the knowledge and skills they need to become financially independent from a young age so that they can continue our legacy and so that they don't fall into the common capitalism-driven consumer trap.

For many first-time parents, the question becomes, when is the appropriate age to start teaching kids about money? The answer is: They're never too young. Small children are remarkably curious but also incredibly impressionable, and instilling sound financial wisdom, like the value of money and savings and introducing them to risk-free investments can prove invaluable.

As our kids grow older, we can begin to have open discussions about money, teach them about work, how to manage debt properly, build a healthy credit score, and gift them a Roth IRA once they have earned enough money from working.

Above all else, we should encourage children to commit to a life that embraces financial literacy and encourages them to think outside of the box so that they're learning from their own experiences and not being brainwashed by systems that are setting them up to fail. We can provide our children with an adequate safety net without outright protecting them from financial mistakes that will teach them valuable lessons. And in teaching our kids, we may end up learning how to pivot and become financially agile ourselves.

The Next Phase of Life

As we enter the next phase of life, we need to continue planning, not just for unforeseen expenses but also for new milestones we will reach. Marriage, starting a family, teaching our kids about financial literacy, investment, retirement, and many other life events will require financial wisdom, continued awareness of consumerism and capitalism, and keeping up with changing markets.

While we can certainly be prepared for what's to come, we need to acknowledge that agility and being open to new perspectives while holding on to tried and tested financial wellness tools, like compound interest, will guide us safely through these new life phases.

Personal Finance Highlights

By embracing mentorship roles, charting clear financial roadmaps, understanding the realities of homeownership, navigating the mortgage process wisely, and evaluating the pros and cons of renting versus owning, individuals can confidently navigate the milestones of adulthood and secure their financial well-being in the ever-changing landscape of consumerism and capitalism.

1. Navigating Adulthood's Financial Maze: As our adult children approach significant milestones like home ownership and starting families, they face unique challenges in today's economic landscape. From soaring home prices to the burden of college debt, young adults must navigate a complex financial maze. By focusing on long-term financial goals rather than societal expectations, they can chart a course towards financial stability and independence.

2. Financial Roadmap: Today's young adults face unique challenges, including rising home prices, student debt, and stagnant wages. Crafting a comprehensive financial roadmap that prioritizes career goals, emergency savings,

retirement planning, and debt management is essential for achieving long-term financial stability.

3. Redefining Home Ownership: The traditional path to homeownership may seem out of reach for many young adults amidst a competitive real estate market. However, by exploring alternative approaches such as purchasing multi-family units or partnering with others, aspiring homeowners can carve out a viable path towards owning property. Flexibility and creativity are key in adapting to the changing dynamics of the housing market.

4. Saving Strategically for Big Purchases: Whether it's saving for a down payment on a home or financing a new vehicle, strategic saving is essential. By leveraging tools like Certificate Deposits (CDs), diversifying income streams, and prioritizing debt repayment, individuals can accelerate their journey toward achieving their financial goals. Patience and discipline are key virtues in building a solid financial foundation.

5. Renting vs. Owning: The decision between renting and owning a home involves weighing various factors, including flexibility, stability, and financial implications. While renting offers agility and fixed costs, homeownership provides equity building and long-term stability. It's essential to evaluate personal priorities and financial goals when making this decision.

CONCLUSION: THE PERSONAL FINANCE CHOICE IS YOURS

As we conclude this book, and perhaps the phase of our lives, we can begin to see how tangled in capitalism and consumerism most of us have become. Reflecting on the knowledge we have learned throughout this book can be used not only to build wealth and financial freedom but also to continue to free ourselves of consumerism's grip and reduce the financial inequality gap.

A solid understanding of the basics like income, expenditure, credit, and effective budgeting is the very bare minimum required to stay afloat. Knowing how to save effectively, manage our debt, and steer clear of credit traps begins to narrow the gap between financial literacy and financial independence. And, once we understand the value of frugal living, investment, and diversifying our income, true financial independence and freedom are within reach.

Always keep in mind that true financial independence requires both financial literacy (education) and financial capability (action). Taking action, committing to saving, choosing to start small, and prioritizing paying off debt when coupled with the knowledge we've learned is the key to building enough wealth to scale up our confidence and move into investing our money wisely.

As our financial independence unfolds, we can begin to embrace the certainties and uncertainties of our futures with confidence in the plans we have laid and the continued action we have taken.

The power of financial choice is our ability to make educated and informed decisions about our financial resources. It's the power to spend, save, invest, and allocate funds in a way that aligns with our goals, values, and priorities rather than being subconscious puppets to the seven percent and consumer culture. It represents the freedom and control to make informed and intentional financial decisions.

The control and responsibility for how money is managed and spent rests with the person or entity that owns the money. Ultimately, the money we make is subject to the decisions we make. Own it. Go and possess it. It's yours to obtain!

Dear Reader,

Your thoughts matter. By sharing your experiences and opinions, you're not only contributing to the ongoing conversation about financial literacy but also shaping the future for generations to come.

Your review of <u>The Personal Finance Choice for Teens and Young Adults</u> holds immense power. Robert F. Newkirk Jr.'s comprehensive guide empowers young minds to master money management and gain financial independence. Thank you for reading this work and thank you for spreading the word!

Respectfully,

Robert F. Newkirk Jr.

REFERENCES

American Psychological Association. (2022). *Stress in America.* https://www.apa.org/news/press/releases/stress/2022/march-2022-survival-mode

Angelou, M. (2019). *Maya Angelou quote.* Goodreads. https://www.goodreads.com/quotes/7273813-do-the-best-you-can-until-you-know-better-then

Bankrate. (2022, November 9). *Understanding car depreciation.* Bankrate. https://www.bankrate.com/insurance/car/understanding-car-depreciation/#:~

Batdorf, E. (2024, February 15). *Majority of Americans live paycheck to paycheck.* Forbes.com. https://www.forbes.com/advisor/banking/living-paycheck-to-paycheck-statistics-2024/

Beyonce. (2018, June 18). *Boss Song* [Song]. Parkwood Entertainment, Sony Music and Roc Nation.

Bezos, J. (n.d.). *Jeff Bezos quotes.* BrainyQuote. https://www.brainyquote.com/quotes/jeff_bezos_449981

Bloomenthal, A. (2022, March 18). *Can a family survive on the U.S. minimum wage?* Investopedia. https://www.investopedia.com/articles/personal-finance/022615/can-family-survive-us-minimum-wage.asp

Bover, O., Hospido, L., & Villanueva, E. (2018). The impact of high school financial education on financial knowledge and choices: evidence from a randomized trial in Spain. *SSRN Electronic Journal.* https://doi.org/10.2139/ssrn.3116054

Brackett, C. (2021, March 9). *How many jobs should I apply to?* LinkedIn. https://www.linkedin.com/pulse/how-many-jobs-should-i-apply-charles-brackett-he-him-

Brown, J. E. (2018, March 7). *Millennials and retirement: Already falling short.* National Institute on Retirement Security. https://www.nirsonline.org/reports/millennials-and-retirement-already-falling-short/

Capitalism. (n.d.) In *Online Etymology Dictionary.* Retrieved on March 21, 2024, fromhttps://www.etymonline.com/word/capitalism#etymonline_v_27665

Choose Fi Foundation. (2021, October 27). *Scary financial literacy statistics for kids, teens & adults (2021).* https://www.choosefifoundation.org/blog/scary%20financial%20literacy%20statistics

Claybourne, C. (2024, January 3). *Alternatives to college: What to know.* U.S. News. https://www.usnews.com/education/best-colleges/articles/alternatives-to-a-4-year-college-what-to-know

Clear, J. (2018). *Atomic habits: tiny changes, remarkable results: an easy & proven way to build good habits & break bad ones.* Avery, An Imprint Of Penguin Random House.

Confucius. (n.d.). *Confucius quotes.* BrainyQuote. https://www.brainyquote.com/quotes/confucius_140908

Douglas, D. (2019). *Work during college: Assessing the impact of student work during college.* https://educpattewell.commons.gc.cuny.edu/files/2019/12/Douglas-and-Attewell_Work-During-College_Rutgers.pdf

du Bois, W. E. B. (n.d.). *W. E. B. du Bois quotes.* Brainy Quote. https://www.brainyquote.com/authors/w-e-b-du-bois-quotes

Edwards, W. (2023, June 22). *Harvard researchers share 7 charts that show the struggles of buying and renting a home in America today, and their recommendations for solving them.* Business Insider. https://www.businessinsider.com/affordable-homes-buying-house-right-now-prices-mortgage-rates-harvard-2023-6#:~

Fay, B. (2022, February 23). *Consumer debt statistics & demographics in America.* Debt.org. https://www.debt.org/faqs/americans-in-debt/demographics/

Feeny, C. (2023, June 29). *5 reasons it's hard to buy a home in the U.S.* Catherine Feeny. https://catherinefeeny.com/why-buy-a-home-in-the-u-s/

Fernandes, D., Lynch, J. G., & Netemeyer, R. G. (2014). Financial literacy, financial education, and downstream financial behaviors. *Management Science, 60*(8), 1861–1883. https://doi.org/10.1287/mnsc.2013.1849

Field, B. (2019). *Financial illiteracy definition: Top definitions of financial illiteracy.* NFEC. https://www.financialeducatorscouncil.org/financial-illiteracy-definition/

Fincher, D. (Director). (2010). *The social network* [Film]. Columbia Pictures, Sony Pictures Releasing France, Sony Pictures Releasing.

Finkelstein, N., & Wright, C. (2023, January 28). *The inspiring outrage of Norman Finkelstein.* Commondreams. https://www.commondreams.org/opinion/the-inspiring-outrage-of-norman-finkelstein

Gay, C. (2024, January 3). *What happened to Claudine Gay.* The NY Times. https://www.nytimes.com/2024/01/03/opinion/claudine-gay-harvard-president.html#:~

Gillespie, L. (2023, February 23). *Bankrate's annual emergency fund report.* Bankrate. https://www.bankrate.com/banking/savings/emergency-savings-report/

Graduate Center, & Office of Communications and Marketing. (2023, November 6). *Behind the U.S. labor strikes.* GC Cuny Edu. https://www.gc.cuny.edu/news/behind-us-labor-strikes

Hanna, K. (2022, March 2). *Finding financial confidence in the journey, not the destination.* Making Your Money Matter. https://www.makingyourmoneymatter.com/financial-freedom-journey/

Hanson, M. (2023, November 28). *Student financial aid statistics.* Education Data. https://educationdata.org/financial-aid-statistics

Hensley, Billy. J. (2019, June 13). *Opinion: Stop the tired argument asserting financial education doesn't work.* NEFE. https://www.nefe.org/news/2019/06/opinion-stop-argument-fin-ed-does-not-work.aspx

Horymski, C. (2024, February 14). *Experian study: Average U.S. consumer debt and statistics.* Experian. https://www.experian.com/blogs/ask-experian/research/consumer-debt-study/

Investor Tools. (2023). *Compound interest calculator.* Investor.gov. https://www.investor.gov/financial-tools-calculators/calculators/compound-interest-calculator

Jemison. M. (n.d.). *Mae Jemison quotes.* Quote Fancy. https://quotefancy.com/quote/1548352/Mae-Jemison-Greatness-can-be-captured-in-one-word-lifestyle-Life-is-God-s-gift-to-you#:~

Johnson, M. (2023a, May 17). *Guilt, dirty money, and their impact on consumer psychology.* Neuroscience Of. https://www.neuroscienceof.com/branding-blog/guilt-consumer-psychology-dirty-money

Johnson, H. (2023b, September 6). *How much free college aid are students missing out on?* Investopedia. https://www.investopedia.com/free-college-aid-missed-5324800

Johnson, H. (2024, January 25). *How long does it take to pay off student loan debt?* Investopedia. https://www.investopedia.com/how-long-pay-off-student-loan-debt-8549844#:~

Johnson, J. H. (n.d.). Quote. In BooKey. (n.d.). *30 best John H Johnson quotes with image.* BooKey. https://www.bookey.app/quote-author/john-h-johnson

Kaur, H., & Kaur, R. (2016). *Effects of materialism on well-being: A review.* https://oaji.net/articles/2016/1170-1468259824.pdf

Kimbro, D. (2013). *The wealth choice.* St. Martin's Press.

Kimbro, D. (n.d.). Quote. In Croxton, S. (n.d.). Dr. Dennis Kimbro. Sean Croxton. https://seancroxton.com/quote-of-the-day/1825/

Klapper, L., Lusardi, A., & Van Oudheusden, P. (2015). *Financial literacy around the world: Insights from the standard and ratings service global financial literacy survey.* https://gflec.org/wp-content/uploads/2015/11/Finlit_paper_16_F2_singles.pdf

Knueven, L., & Grace, M. (2024, January 2). *The average monthly mortgage payment by state, city, and year.* Business Insider. https://www.businessinsider.com/personal-finance/average-mortgage-payment#:~

Lach, L., & Nzorubara, D. (2023, April 17). *The cost of financial illiteracy.* IFAC. https://www.ifac.org/knowledge-gateway/contributing-global-economy/discussion/cost-financial-illiteracy

Louis, S. (2024, January 5). *"Millions of Americans are retiring with no savings": Study shows about 90% of low-income households have nothing stashed away for retirement — here's how to catch up.* Yahoo Finance. https://finance.yahoo.com/news/millions-americans-retiring-no-savings-123000477.html

Madison, C. (2021, January 27). *Teens against consumerism–the anti-excess movement.* Voices of Youth. https://www.voicesofyouth.org/blog/teens-against-consumerism-anti-excess-movement#:

Magett, Carole Elyse, Robert A. Esperti, Reno L. Peterson, (1996), *Legacy: Plan, Protect, & Preserve Your Estate,* pp 182-187, The Institute Inc.

Malik, F., & Ishaq, M. I. (2023). Impact of minimalist practices on consumer happiness and financial well-being. *Journal of Retailing and Consumer Services, 73,* 103333. https://doi.org/10.1016/j.jretconser.2023.103333

Mandela. N. (2019). *Nelson Mandela quotes.* BrainyQuote. https://www.brainyquote.com/Authors/Nelson-Mandela-Quotes

McCreary, R. (2018, March 14). *Financial literacy and capitalism.* CW Industrial Partners. https://cwindustrials.com/financial-literacy-and-capitalism/

Marder, A. (2023, May 30). *Most Americans have a monthly budget, but many still overspend.* NerdWallet. https://www.nerdwallet.com/article/finance/data-2023-budgeting-report

Menard, M. (2017). So many courses, so little progress: Why financial education doesn't work - And what does. *SSRN Electronic Journal.* https://doi.org/10.2139/ssrn.3098279

Murphy, C. B. (2024, February 24). *Debt-to-Income (DTI) ratio: Definition and formula.* Investopedia. https://www.investopedia.com/terms/d/dti.asp#:~

Next Gen Personal Finance. (2022). *State of financial education report 2021-2022.* https://www.ngpf.org/state-of-fin-ed-report-2021-2022/

New King James Version. (n.d.). *Proverbs 22 NIV.* Bible Hub https://biblehub.com/niv/proverbs/22.htm

Obel, M. (2023, October 23). *What is the average student loan interest rate and payment?* Smart Asset. https://smartasset.com/student-loans/average-student-loan-interest-rate#:~

Ogden, T. (2019, April 23). More states are forcing students to study personal finance. It's a waste of time. *The Washington Post.* https://www.washingtonpost.com/outlook/2019/04/23/more-states-are-forcing-students-study-personal-finance-its-waste-time/

Perna, M. C. (2021, November 1). *$100 million in scholarship money goes unclaimed every year. Does it have to?* Forbes. https://www.forbes.com/sites/markcperna/2021/11/01/100-million-in-scholarship-money-goes-unclaimed-every-year-does-it-have-to/

Piette, B. (2023, January 27). *Capitalist system cause of wealth inequality.* Workers World. https://www.workers.org/2023/01/68835/

Poole. J. H. (n.d.). *John. H. Poole quotes.* Quote Fancy. www.quotefancy.com/quote/1718145/H-John-Poole-You-must-learn-to-save-first-and-spend-afterwards

Raghuram Rajan, & Zingales, L. (2003). *Saving capitalism from the capitalists: Unleashing the power of financial markets to create wealth and spread opportunity.* Princeton University Press.

Reinicke, C. (2020, December 9). *Teens call for more personal finance education to bridge economic opportunity gap in America.* CNBC. https://www.cnbc.com/2020/12/09/teens-need-more-finance-education-to-bridge-economic-gap-in-america.html

Rivera, H. (2023, July 26). *College tuition inflation.* Bankrate. https://www.bankrate.com/loans/student-loans/college-tuition-inflation/#:~

Robbins, A. (2016). *Money: master the game: 7 simple steps to financial freedom.* Simon & Schuster Paperbacks.

Rosales, J. M. (2023, December 26). *Harmony in hustle: 20 quotes to inspire work-life balance.* Accounting Professor. https://accountingprofessor.org/harmony-in-hustle-20-quotes-to-inspire-work-life-balance/

Schulz, M. (2023, August 10). *U.S. student loan debt statistics for 2023.* LendingTree. https://www.lendingtree.com/student/student-loan-debt-statistics/

Spenser, H. (nd). *Spenser Quotes.* BrainyQuote. https://www.brainyquote.com/quotes/herbert_spencer_109568

Stoll, T. (2023). *Financial literacy survey.* NFEC. https://www.financialeducatorscouncil.org/financial-literacy-survey/?gad_source=1&gclid=Cj0KCQiAtaOtBhCwARIsAN_x-3Jjb9ZP8IlDWILQSCCdi8OrhA0DTELTI_xiCXY2l8YlDWW3jO7ZP7saAsNGEALw_wcB

Tough, P. (2023, September 5). *Americans are losing faith in the value of college. Whose fault is that?.* The New York Times. https://www.nytimes.com/2023/09/05/magazine/college-worth-price.html

Tucker, S. (2023, May 16). *Average American car now 12.5 years old.* Kelley Blue Book. https://www.kbb.com/car-news/average-american-car-now-12-5-years-old/

U.S. Bureau of Labor Statistics. (2024). *Employment status of the civilian noninstitutional population, 1944 to date.* https://www.bls.gov/cps/aa2014/cpsaat01.htm

Wagatha, E., & Chen, V. (2023, August 31). *GenZ and Millennial consumers: What defines them and what divides them.* GFK. https://www.gfk.com/blog/gen-z-and-millennial-consumers-what-defines-them-and-what-divides-them

Wallace, A. (2023, August 8). *Americans' credit card debt hits a record $1 trillion.* CNN.

https://www.cnn.com/2023/08/08/economy/us-household-credit-card-debt/index.html

Wertz, J. (2018, October 28). *How to win over Generation Z, who hold $44 billion of buying power*. Forbes. https://www.forbes.com/sites/jiawertz/2018/10/28/how-to-win-over-generation-z-who-hold-44-billion-of-buying-power/

Ziglar. (2015, August 25). *The ladder of success*. https://www.ziglar.com/quotes/you-cannot-climb-the-ladder-of-success/

Zippia. (2023, January 11). *Average number of jobs in a lifetime [2023]: How many jobs does the average person have?* https://www.zippia.com/advice/average-number-jobs-in-lifetime

Made in United States
Troutdale, OR
12/17/2024

26653297R10117